D1569221

Letters of Henry Miller and Wallace Fowlie

HENRY MILLER

Letters of
Henry Miller
and
Wallace Fowlie
(1943-1972)

by Henry Miller and Wallace Fowlie

With an Introduction
by Wallace Fowlie

Grove Press, Inc., New York

ISBN: 0–394–49737–6
Grove Press ISBN: 0–8021–0072–4

Library of Congress Catalog Card Number: 74–24859

First Printing

Manufactured in the United States of America

Distributed by Random House, Inc.

GROVE PRESS, INC., 53 East 11th Street, New York, New York 10003

Contents

Introduction
by Wallace Fowlie

WALLACE FOWLIE

With Henry Miller I have had an epistolary and literary friendship. Most of the letters we exchanged were written between 1943 and 1950. During approximately four of those years his letters were important to me in many ways. They encouraged me in the writing I was trying to do. For the first time a man of letters, whom I did not know and whose work I admired, had taken the trouble to write to me about one of my essays. Then, as time went on and our correspondence grew, he continued to show interest, to criticize, to approve, to encourage. Heretofore, friends and teachers had helped and guided me. But with Henry Miller the experience was new and overwhelming. Each existed for the other as writer. He was well known and I was practically unknown.

The literary relationship remained, but a warm friendship grew out of it. This story is in the letters which Henry has permitted me to publish. Their value lies in several matters that are outside our personal relationship: literary opinions, biographical facts, attitudes both spiritual and humanistic. The rhythm of the sentences, their candor, the humor and poignancy of many passages, seem to justify publication. A letter of Henry Miller, no matter how brief, is unmistakably his own, and yet it always reveals an awareness of the friend to whom he is writing. And that is why each collection of letters already published reveals a different Henry Miller concentrated on problems and views associated with his correspondent. He is a universal man, whose range of interests and sympathies is vast. As he liked to say about Rabelais, one of his favorite writers, I would say about him: human to the core — the best rounded writer we have. . . .

The opening letter explains the beginning of our friendship. The first actual commission to write an article had come to me in the summer of 1943, from *View,* the surrealist magazine in New York. The two young editors Charles Henri Ford and Parker Tyler had extended the invitation by suggesting a topic that seemed beyond my powers. I had just completed an essay on the theme of "Narcissus" and, knowing it to be a favorite preoccupation with surrealists, sent it to *View.* It was accepted, and appeared, with illustrations, as the lead article of an issue.

Soon after its appearance I received a letter from Henry Miller expressing interest in the article. A modest postscript informed me that he had published two books in Paris. One of my students at Bennington College had a year or two earlier shown me *Tropic of Cancer,* and I had also read one of his books published in this country, *The Cosmological Eye.* Both books had left a deep impression. So, we struck up a correspondence. His letters contained a warm friendliness and enthusiasm, an eagerness to converse and discuss, a total freshness of approach to books. Stray remarks of Henry about a book would turn me back to it with revitalized curiosity.

His letters were frequent and long. They made him into a very real person for me, a friend equally solicitous about problems of writing and about the diverse facts of existence. In these letters his personality became so strong and pervasive that I felt it would never be necessary to meet him. Just at that time, in the fall of 1944, when I was teaching at Yale, and living in Trumbull College as resident fellow, he announced his arrival in New Haven, and his desire to stay a few days with me.

I knew very well that a personality contained in correspondence (mine at any rate) is quite different from a personality in the flesh. I was eager to see Henry Miller and to talk with him directly, but what had already transpired between us was so vibrant and salutary that I dreaded any diminution, any risk of failure. After a few minutes with him, I realized that the experience of knowing him personally was to provide me with a further illumination on mankind and a further strengthening of friendship.

I had been expecting his arrival all one morning. Late in the morning he telephoned from Bridgeport and said he would get in about two. Exactly at two o'clock, the bell rang. He was standing in the hall, so alone and so quietly withdrawn into himself, that my first impression of him in the second before we spoke, was his independence and separation from the world. He asked for me, and when he learned that I was the friend he had come to see, he expressed surprise at not recognizing me, at not finding me what he had expected — a much older man.

He had not had lunch, and I invited him into the kitchen while I set about making coffee and scrambling eggs. This delighted him. He said, "This is exactly what I would have done for you if you had landed at my place." I found it difficult to scramble eggs and talk at the same time, but gradually Henry put me at ease. His voice was low and exceptionally resonant. It gave great clarity to whatever he said. While I continued to blurt out inconsequential sentences, he never wasted a word. Each phrase he uttered was poised and precisely filled some function. What helped me the most was his sentence spoken soon after I had begun the lunch preparations, when my mind was still more on the opening conversation than on the kitchen gestures: "What about that coffee you promised me?"

When we finally settled down in the living room, he spoke with that deepest kind of grace that comes from a concern with what is most central in the person addressed. Henry fixed himself comfortably in a large chair and then said with a smile of contentment and expectancy, "Now tell me all about *acedia*." I was prepared for almost anything but that. He explained that he had come across the word for the first time in one of my essays and had been fascinated by it.

In reply, I actually said very little, but he seized upon it and began developing it himself. Henry needed no teacher. Just a few words of suggestion were enough and he began explaining the subject to himself out loud. He literally appropriated the term *acedia* and then composed for it a new setting and a new meaning. I followed both the transformation of the word and the exhilaration of the man who played as he created and learned. The tedious method of teaching was completely surpassed in that joyous process which combined intellect and imagination. Somehow in Henry Miller the art of learning is carried out by immediacy, by an act of love, a joining of himself with the subject. And then abruptly, as if, when the act had been consummated, everything changed. What was learned, was abandoned. Something else solicited him, another word or a thought; and the joyous expectancy, at once so childlike and so profound, filled him until the desire became imperious and demanded satisfaction.

One of my students, Jesse Clark, had pleaded more insistently than the others, to meet Miller, and I arranged for him to come in on the second afternoon. Jess had been a civilian student of mine first and then had changed into an apprentice seaman in the V-12 program. He had continued with French as an additional luxury to his navy courses. Of all my students that year he had distinguished himself to me by a temperament and imagination which I recognized as being those of an artist. Our conversations had centered on the life of a writer, on how he exists, on how he feels the world and controls it. Jess had shown me passages in his diary that were explosions against the world and against himself.

I remember Jess sitting down in his chair very soberly and quietly — there was great dignity in his posture and appearance, as there was great fire and animation in his speech. At first he spoke reservedly to Henry. I had tried to "explain" Jess before he came in, and saw immediately that all explanations had been unnecessary. Henry turned his attention on the boy as if a bond of understanding existed between them. He spoke to him as an equal and listened to whatever remarks Jess offered.

At one point, Henry turned abruptly to me and said, referring to Jess, "His head is just like Van Gogh's. Have you ever noticed the resemblance? And his hands are those of a painter."

In recalling the two weeks Henry Miller spent at New Haven, I have no impression of a sequence of days. It was a long conversation in multiple parts with multiple interruptions. His kindness and attentiveness were overwhelming. I had never before observed a man able to remain so alert and fervent in every aspect of living and thinking. Through simple proximity, I felt a new vigor in myself. I was aware those weeks of recasting and reassessing themes and problems of my entire life. Many strands seemed to be joining together. I almost caught sight of a unity in living. Whether we talked of Rimbaud or the circus, of Chaplin or D. H. Lawrence, of films, of Paris, the subjects all fused.

Marguerite and Henri Peyre came to my apartment at Trumbull the first afternoon. I was pleased to bring about this meeting because Peyre had been one of the first critics in this country to praise Miller as a writer and to point out his importance. The conversation was lively and rich although Henri Peyre wanted to concentrate on Henry Miller's reactions to America on his recent return from France, and Miller, in the presence of an authentic Frenchman, wanted to revive his memories of Paris and discuss the writings of Blaise Cendrars and Céline, yes, and even Rabelais. Marguerite Peyre seemed to be delighted with Miller's attitudes and reflections. I was confirmed in my belief that she enjoyed the company of writers more than that of academics.

Gradually word circulated that Henry Miller was at Yale, and staying at the resident fellow's apartment at Trumbull. Henry gave in to my request that he talk with a few groups of students — four or five at a time. He was cordial with them and infinitely patient in answering their questions. He promised to sell, at an insignificant price, a few of his water-colors to some students he especially enjoyed talking with: Jesse Clark, Harvey Buchanan, David Sudarsky.

Then invitations for lunch came from other colleges, from the master or from students. Jonathan Edwards College, in particular, I remember, welcomed Henry in royal fashion. Finally, as the ultimate homage, a letter came to him in my mailbox from President Seymour, inviting him to give a public lecture and offering an honorarium of one thousand dollars. Henry read the letter to me and quietly said: "If anyone needs that dough, I do, but I've never given a lecture and I never will. You can always invite a few friends here to Trumbull and I'll talk to them." As I listened to his reaction to the president's letter, my admiration for Henry Miller reached a new peak.

A number of days went by before Henry introduced me to a new friend of his, Martha Lepska, a graduate student in philosophy at Yale. Then one evening the three of us went to the movies, and talked afterwards. I suspected that Henry was serious about Lepska, as he called her, and the day he left New Haven (I was busy teaching all that morning) I found a letter from him, written in French, when I got back to Trumbull. It was, in reality, an announcement of his intention to marry this very gifted and very charming young Polish girl.

My initial debt to Henry came from the encouragement he had given to my writing before he knew me personally. Then, after our meeting, a new debt became apparent to me, and has not ceased growing ever since: an awareness of that unity he feels in himself which he is able in part to transmit to his friends. Whatever act or detail about myself turned up in the conversation, Henry immediately interpreted so eloquently and convincingly that I believed I existed in a cosmos invisible to me heretofore.

With Henry's departure, apartment 1248 recovered its solitude. My steps, as I walked down the hall, actually echoed. I continued seeing him move lithely from room to room, and I continued hearing him marvel at the austerity of the building. "How can you stand it? How can you stand it?" he used to say, speaking almost to himself.

I believe the quality that first attracted me to Henry Miller's writings was his violence. Not the violence of the things said, but the violence of the way in which they were said. The violence of feeling has become in his work the violence of style which has welded together all of his disparate passions and dispersed experiences into the one experience of language. He has said in *The Wisdom of the Heart* that he doesn't believe in words, but in language, "which is something beyond words." Writing is a complete celebration for him in which shattered parts of experience are put together, in which elements are fused. These elements are not, however, fused into a system of thought and experience which can be learned or understood. They can only be "realized," more and more intuitively. Miller reveals in his art the gift of immediacy. His hungers of the present are never over. They never become past hungers to be recalled. From his vision of life, which is one self-perpetuating experience, comes his writing, integrated with the flowing steadiness of life, pulsating with the sameness of each day, incapable of being codified and explicated in accordance with the rules of "periods," of "genres," of "themes."

Henry Miller is a leading example of a special kind of writer who is essentially seer and prophet, whose immediate ancestor was Rimbaud and whose leading exponent was D. H. Lawrence. It is not insignificant that he considers the poet whose perceptions and visions blotted out his language — Arthur Rimbaud — one of the greatest writers. What characterizes this kind of writer is his vulnerability to experiences. He exposes himself to them all in a propitiatory frenzy. In a more histrionic sense, this artist is the scapegoat who feels physically the weight of the world's sins and who performs in his life the role of the clown. He relives all the incarnations of the hero which he calls, in his more modest language, his masks. Miller was also fascinated by the names Rimbaud used for himself in *Une saison en enfer: saltimbanque, mendiant, artiste, bandit, prêtre* (acrobat, beggar, artist, bandit, priest).

The reasons for this reduplicated role of the artist are difficult to state because they are so deeply imbedded in the spiritual problems of our age which, although they explain us, do not always explain themselves to us. Beginning with *The Tropic of Cancer* in 1934, and continuing in all of his writings through the most recent pamphlet, *On Turning Eighty*, of 1972, Henry Miller has been writing his autobiography, and at the same time the history of our age. In his frank acceptance of the world, he learned to perceive in it the forces of evil as well as the forces of good, and hence to prepare himself for the particular role of prophet which he has played so consistently and so brilliantly.

The very title of Mr. Miller's book, *The Wisdom of the Heart*, is a key to the artist's function, and in it, on page 45, there is a sentence that might well be a text to explain all of his books: "We are in the grip of demonic forces created by our own fear and ignorance." The little man who is terrified, and who is in reality greater than that which terrifies him, is the choreographic objectification of the artist. He is the homunculus who is physically crushed by the world but who spiritually dominates the world in his quest for the absolute. The heroes whom Henry Miller talks about the most often are all the same type of passionate clown: Rimbaud and Lawrence, Chaplin and Raimu, Christ and Saint Francis, Miller himself as hero in *The Tropic of Cancer*. When he writes about the French, it is always about the little man, the insignificant man, but who is the microcosmic representation of the age: the *garçon de café*, the store proprietor, the whore, the pimp.

On the homunculus falls more lucidly than on the proud and successful the shadow of doom announced by Spengler and Lawrence. Henry Miller continued the prophetic role of those two writers but preached less. Oswald Spengler, the prophet of cyclical history, D. H. Lawrence, the psychologist of love and sex, and Henry Miller, the visionary who perceives his wisdom in the microcosm of the heart, are all contained in the boy-prophet Arthur Rimbaud.

The prophet or the visionary is the man who daily lives the metaphysical problems of his age. How to live is the theme of all prophets. Peace is always the goal; and around the word "peace" cluster the plans and the dreams, the intuitions and the burning designs of those men who see into the heart of the living and into the future. The peace of the world is, for Henry Miller, associated with Paris, because there it is more possible for man, so divided in his natural heritages, to become one as artist.

In their creative activity, even if not always in their lives as men, some of the most notable among contemporary artists have attained a unity thanks to the spiritual role of Paris. It is impossible to measure the peace of Paris in the work of Frenchmen like Proust, Breton, Rouault; of the Irish James Joyce; of the Russian Chagall and Tchelitchev; of the Spanish

Picasso; of the American Gertrude Stein, Hemingway, and Henry Miller. From some wellspring of ancient liberty, Paris has safeguarded a fertile power in the unity of her native and assimilated artists who, not only in the accomplishment of their work but in their understanding of man, defy the usual contemporary waywardness and bifurcations.

Throughout the history of American literature, there has been an uninterrupted preoccupation with the theme of evil, treated from a special viewpoint of horror and awesomeness and fixation. Poe, Melville, Djuna Barnes, and Julien Green in his French novels, are united in their conception of evil as being a sense of dark foreboding and the plotting of malign spirits. I believe that the work of Henry Miller (and by "work" I mean his presence, his spirit, and the profoundest meaning of his books) has interrupted the traditional American treatment of evil. The obvious reason for Miller's books not being published in America during the 40's and 50's is the obscenity of their language in some of the passages. But this violence was needed to redirect the American consciousness of evil. The obscenity in the two *Tropics* is a form of medication and catharsis, an extroversion needed after all the books of puritanical foreboding. Both Miller's dissoluteness in language and his fixation on the physical possession of woman were means of liberating himself from the Hamlet-soul which has dominated the American literary heroes during the long period between the revolution of 1789 and World War II. Miller's were *the* pioneer books in the freedom of language and attitudes toward sex in American books and films since the 1960's.

"And always I am hungry," Henry Miller writes in *The Wisdom of the Heart*. Alimentary and sexual hunger are one kind, and spiritual hunger is another. Both are centrally analyzed in Miller's books. The long line of heroes extending from Hamlet to Charlie Chaplin who have been awkward in the presence of woman and unable to express themselves in love, have developed in woman a false role of domination which D. H. Lawrence was among the first to castigate. Lawrence was devoted to love, and Miller is devoted to life, but both have expressed fear of woman's role in the modern world and her usurping of man's position. Hence their treatment of woman, in order to undermine her role of mother for her husband and of frigid goddess for her lover. Lawrence treats woman as wife who is essentially mistress, and Miller often treats woman as prostitute. Their use of woman, rather than restoring her to her natural role, has become just one other perversion, comparable to man's excessive love for his mother, as in Proust, and his excessive hate for his mother, as in Rimbaud.

Henry Miller knows that there is no solution to the problem of man's sexual hunger. He writes in his book, *The World of Sex*, "I am essentially a religious person, and always have been." In the Paris television interview he gave to Georges Belmont in 1969, he said: "I am fundamentally a religious man without a religion. I believe in the existence of a supreme intelligence. Call it God if you wish." Flashes everywhere in his writing testify to a sensitivity that worships. Every action and every word, no matter how seemingly inconsequential, has a meaning for him and a part in the wholeness of things. The visionary is always akin to the religious, because to see the plenitude of the cosmos is to love it and to accept it. To read Henry Miller has always been for me to discover a kind of peace in the world. He is the one contemporary writer who has driven out from his nature all traces of hamletism, and yet he writes constantly about Hamlet. About Hamlet as death-sower.

All the aspects of Miller's art and his nature are unified. He is one person, one visionary. But his vision is multiple and changing and even contradictory. That is as it should be. Love is something else and Miller has defined it admirably in *The World of Sex*: "Love is the drama of completion, of unification." The purpose of life attracts him more than the complexities of any single existence. In his vision, details and debts are forgotten, and he sees only the dark results of corruption and the blazing projects of rejuvenation.

Despite his fame today, despite the notable success of his books throughout the world, Henry Miller at the age of eighty-three still tends to think of himself as a failure, *un raté*, as he said to Georges Belmont in the television interview. He identifies with the poor, the wretched, the unknown of the world. He has often spoken of his attraction to the story of D. H. Lawrence, concerning Jesus after the resurrection when he returns to earth and appears as an ordinary man, nondescript, almost an idiot. But that is when Jesus enjoyed life and found it exhilarating. If Miller himself is reincarnated and returns to the earth in another form, he hopes he will be a nobody, the most humble of men, unknown, and without an occupation.

In another age, he would have been a gnostic or a monk, and leading the kind of life in which all the contradictions of his nature would be explained and harmonized. Those friends who have perhaps understood him the best: Lawrence Durrell, Anaïs Nin, Brassai, Perlès, William Carlos Williams, in their praise have always spoken of the good influence he has been in the world, of his simplicity and honesty, of his ability to find himself the same man in his roles of clown and angel, the same man wherever he is living: Brooklyn, Dijon, Big Sur, Paris, Pacific Palisades. He has known suffering and upheavals in his personal life, anguish that brought him close to suicide, but more than most men, he is able to be at peace with himself in the midst of his conflicts. It is less important for Miller to be a writer than to be a man at peace with himself. By most people, he is thought of as the man who wrote the two *Tropics,* and they seldom consider the other lives he has led since that already distant time. His memory, faithful to itself, has become his work. It has continued to unfold and reveal itself in its ever expanding universe.

Henry Miller has always been surprised at his reputation of a writer about sex, and through the years has grown weary of the same question always asked him: "If you consider yourself a religious man, why do you write about sex as you do?" The answer is simple and Miller has repeated it on many occasions. Western civilization, Christianity in many of the forms it has taken, has created a conflict between the body and the spirit, which Henry Miller has never felt. The façades of some of the great temples of India are covered with sculptured bodies of men and women in the most erotic postures that can be imagined. For Miller they are the work of religious spirits for whom sexuality, the worship of the human body, is the way leading to God. He has always looked upon his sexual life as normal and natural. He has written directly about sexual adventures which other men conceal under the words which they use. A close reading of Miller's books will show that actually he is timid in the presence of women. It is they who seduced him.

He admires woman for being more of the earth than he can be. He has often claimed that passion for woman remains personal, whereas man, more religious than woman, is passionate for abstract ideas and for God. Men are in error, he says, when they deliberately fail to cultivate the feminine element of their nature. The world as we know it is run by men, and badly run. Through the ages, man has impressed upon woman that she belongs to one man alone. This seems to Miller the source of much of the turmoil in the world, and nostalgically he thinks of prehistoric times when anthropologists tell us about matriarchies, about woman-dominated civilizations.

We may never learn what daemon inhabits Henry Miller, what spirit has made him into the honest writer that he is. But we do know beyond any doubt that he has remained totally faithful to his daemon. He is incorruptible. He cannot be bought by fame or money. He is more honest than most intellectuals. He has the integrity of a primitive living in a decadent world. He is not an exile from that world, but he is its critic. I would compare him, not so much to Rabelais as many critics have, but to Saint Francis. *Black Spring* is our contemporary "Hymn to the Sun."

It is tempting to compare Miller with Lawrence or Joyce or even Beckett. But there is no point to doing that — he does not possess the architectonic skill of a novelist. He is a world literary figure who has given us the best confessional writing since Jean-Jacques Rousseau. He has given us the best account of a writer's day-dreaming and reveries that are different from those of the layman.

Older than Steinbeck, Dos Passos, Hemingway, and Fitzgerald, he was not a member of the "lost generation" hesitating between exile in Montparnasse and commitment to the grapes of wrath. He has always been the pure singer of individual freedom who was a-political because he believed that to give up a capitalistic regime for a socialist regime was simply to change masters. His personal creed may be attached in part to the European utopia of the noble savage, and in part to the American tradition of the return to nature we read in Thoreau and Whitman. His sense of anarchy is partly that of Thoreau and partly that of the Beat Generation.

Miller is not a writer of pornography. He uses obscenity as a means of expressing natural forces in him that rise up against the constraints of civilization. His liberation begins with the liberation of his sexual drives. Obscenity is his battle cry against the air-conditioned nightmare. If one wanted to read about sex as a thesis, one would read Lawrence and not Miller. If one wanted to read about sex as sensuality, one would read Colette and not Miller. Sex is for Miller the symbol of the violent quest for experience that took him from an ordinary office job in America to the Paris of whores and bistros. He is the archetypal bohemian who to his newest readers today sounds like a sage rather than a tramp or a *clochard.* A young reader who was an adolescent in the decade of the 60's, on reading *Black Spring,* would equate the twenty-page passage "The Angel Is My Watermark" with the best pages of *Leaves of Grass* and *Howl.* He would be held, not so much by the episodes and the anecdotes in the books as by the intermittent explanations Miller is always giving us of what the artist is, as the man who has antennae and knows how to hook up to the currents that are in the cosmos.

The real thinkers of any age, the answerers to the really serious questions of humanity, have always lived as temporary exiles. They gain admittance to the company of the immortals by living just outside the rank of the mortals. During their lifetime they appear to most men as loafers, subversive, cranks, useless, and even dangerous to the establishment. Socrates was one of them, and Baudelaire, Thoreau, Henry Miller. They answer the questions of the few people who come to see them at the edge of Walden Pond, or at the top of Big Sur. They write, they paint, they hack away at the old forms of art and at the old forms of morals.

"Each man," Miller tells us in *Black Spring,* "is his own civilized desert, the island of self on which he is shipwrecked." Each artistic work is a flight off from this island of self, and he alludes to the classic flights of Melville, Rimbaud, Gauguin, Henry James, D. H. Lawrence. "The Angel Is My Watermark" is in one respect a treatise on the surrealist method of composition. In it Miller describes himself painting a watercolor. He feels like a watercolor and then he does one. He begins by drawing a horse. (Miller has vaguely in mind the Etruscan horses he had seen in the Louvre.) At one moment the horse resembles a hammock and then when he adds stripes, it becomes a zebra. He adds a tree, a mountain, an angel, cemetery gates. These are the forms that occur almost unpredictably on his paper. He submits it to the various processes of smudging, of soaking it in the sink, of holding it upside down and letting the colors coagulate. Finally it is done: a masterpiece that has come about by accident. But then Miller says that the Twenty-third Psalm was another accident. He looks at the watercolor and sees it to be the result of mistakes, erasures, hesitations, but also "the result of certitude." Every work of art has to be credited, in some mysterious way, to every artist. So Miller credits Dante, Spinoza, and Hieronymous Bosch for his little watercolor.

The Letters

Note: Explanatory material (first names, geographical locations, etc.) not originally in the letters has been set off within brackets. As little as possible of this has been done, in order to preserve the natural flow of the sentences. — *Ed.*

1212 N. Beverly Glen Bld.
Los Angeles (24) Cal.
Nov. 13th 1943

Dear Mr. Fowlie —

Last night on going to bed I read your piece "Narcissus" in *View*. It is now high noon of the next day and I am looking at it again, still terribly intrigued, still marveling over the way you expressed yourself. It is so seldom that one reads anything in English that has the flavor and quality of your writing. I am dumbfounded and bewildered by the beauty, clarity and profundity of this study. I should like to know where I may obtain your books, both in English and in French. It seems to me you must have been educated in France, perhaps spoke French first.

Have you by chance expanded on this theme — Narcissus — in any of your books?

That reproduction of painting by "master of Paris" also haunts me, especially the image in the pool.

I do hope to hear from you.

Sincerely yours,
Henry Miller

P.S. I lived for a number of years in Paris and was first published there — in English.

1248 Yale Station
New Haven, Conn.
20 Nov. 1943

Dear Mr. Miller,

I have been for some time an admirer of your work and I have often thought of writing a study of your books. You can realize from this the intense pleasure your note gave me. I value your approval of *Narcissus* more highly than I can tell you.

The Tropic of cancer (I haven't been able to see a copy of the other *Tropic*) seems to me an important and powerful novel. And *The Cosmological eye* has stimulated me more than any other book I have read during the past five years.

Thank you very much for being interested in my writing. I am sending you one of the French books, and as soon as the new English book is out, in December, I will send it to you.

The *Narcissus* is a chapter in a new book I am completing now. It is a book on love.

I hope that soon you will be coming back to the east and that we can meet. When I learned you were in New York a little while ago, I was very tempted to get in touch with you — but I felt intimidated about making such a move. It would be good to talk with you about Paris.

Sincerely,
Wallace Fowlie

Nov. 27th 1943

Dear Mr. Fowlie —

Your letter comes as a complete surprise to me — a most delightful one. You can't imagine how impatient I am to read *all*

your books — and especially this one you speak of, "on love."
I wrote "View" to send me a number of copies so that I may
distribute them among my friends. I seem always to be doing
this — recommending unheard of books (my latest passion was
for "Interlinear to Cabeza de Vaca" by Haniel Long).

I only wish I might procure for you a copy of the "Capricorn" which I think is greater than "Cancer" — and which I
am continuing in a second volume to be called "The Rosy
Crucifixion."

I shall only be going East in the event of my mother's death.
Otherwise I turn South — to Mexico. I give you the address, for
future use, of my agents in N.Y. — Russell and Volkening,
522 Fifth Ave. — who would forward my mail. (But I shan't
be leaving here till January, late, or February.)

There are phrases from your "Narcissus" that ring in my
ears. One or two I have written on the walls here. It was an
event for me — reading this. I want more, more. I think you
mentioned (or was it Calas) Otto Rank, whom I knew in Paris.
What a wretched writer he was — for all his illuminating ideas.
How clear and vivid is your writing — and so unpedestrian, if
I may say it thus. Though why do I put it negatively? (I am
only making mental comparisons between you, the poet, and
the analysts, who are all dry bones.)

I mentioned "Capricorn," meaning to add that a book store
man in New Haven — Barrie, *I think* (?) — has a copy, or
did have. Doesn't the Yale Library have one? Most universi-
ties now seem to own a copy — at least so I am told.

Forgive me for speaking of myself, my books — but only
because I believe I may give you pleasure. The book on Greece
— "The Colossus of Maroussi" is obtainable. I do think you
would enjoy it.

Well, I wait feverishly for yours to arrive — and I regard
them, sight unseen, as great gifts. I read little — only what I
desperately long to read. I read Rimbaud over and over.

My very best to you. I am so happy to have found a living writer like you.

Henry Miller

1248 Yale Station
4 Dec. 1943

Dear Mr. Miller,

I wished often this last week that you had been within talking distance. The Office of War Information has asked me to take a job in French propaganda — which may mean leaving in a month for London or North Africa. However, nothing is yet official and nothing is sure. To do this new work would mean eliminating the few precious hours a day I have for my own writing. These last few years have been good fertile years: the book I am finishing now on love (there is only one more chapter to write) is the one I have put most of myself into. Since you liked the Narcissus chapter, I am anxious for you to see other parts. A few of the chapters are coming out in magazines. Do you see *The Chimera*? The chapter on Rimbaud and Crane is coming out in that this month. If you don't receive it, I'll send you a copy.

If I can locate a copy of *Capricorn*, and if it is too expensive, I will urge the Yale Library to buy it. They have the *Cancer*. The book can't circulate. I have often recommended it to students — those capable of appreciating it — and they have to read it in the presence of a blushing female library assistant!

Have you seen the photograph of Rimbaud at twelve, the First Communion photograph? I will send you one if you would like to have it. It is a remarkable picture.

Clowns and Angels is out on the tenth of this month. Your copy will leave New York on that day.

I can't tell you how much good it has done me to know you, Henry Miller, even by correspondence, to know that you are out there, that you care somewhat, and that I can write to you from time to time. I am going to begin now a rereading of all your work. Please believe that I am among your most fervent readers.

Devotedly yours,
Wallace Fowlie

12/12/43

Dear Mr. Fowlie —

There is something in you which delights and excites me. It is a great regret to me also not to be able to communicate more easily and immediately with you. I have met only one man since I am out here who really interested me — a Greek painter from Paris named Jean Varda. I go to spend Xmas with him at Monterey.

Indeed I would love to have a copy of "The Chimaera" (I've never even heard of it) as well as the photograph of Rimbaud you mention. I have on one wall here some most interesting photos — of people. It balances the other walls, which are crowded with my rather lurid water colors. And as for that chapter from your book — and "Clowns and Angels" — yes, yes. Most pleased and touched by your generosity.

I am reading — slowly — the one you already sent. It seems more academic to me than the "Narcissus" piece. But always there are lines and phrases, allusions which touch me off. How you ever got into "View" seems strange to me. But then everything about that review is weird.

Should you ever get to Cairo look up two good friends of mine — you will like them, I believe. Both poets. The one is Lawrence Durrell, who is in the Publicity Section of the British Embassy. The other is George Seferiades [Giorgos Seferis], c/o Greek Legation there. I wish I were going to either London or Cairo. I loathe it here — anywhere in America. I seem to have nothing in common with my compatriots. I like *all* foreigners. They stimulate me. Here I feel as if I were in a tomb.

I doubt, by the way, that you will be able to lay hands on a copy of "Capricorn." But now someone promises to print privately 300 copies of it to sell at $10 the copy. I hope it is true. I am lucky too in that these last few days more friends have appeared and promise to bring out certain unpublished material — in rather unorthodox fashion. Everything has changed materially in last few weeks. I myself went thru a great change — morally, spiritually — about the time I went to Greece. I think I am just about beginning to reap the fruits. Not that I wanted material success. Rather greater opportunity to influence the world for good. Or to put it more properly — to increment the good. In my best moments I see it all as being good, right, just — wouldn't change it by a hair. Those are the true moments.

Yes, do keep in touch with me wherever you go. I feel drawn to you.

Henry Miller

P. S. I came over from Greece on the same boat with Jacques Maritain. Sat at next table to his. Never addressed a word to him — tho' I was dying to. Shyness. Often it's that way. The very ones you wish to know, the only ones you care about, you never approach.

---

28 Dec. 1943

Dear Henry Miller,

Perhaps you have received by now the copy of *Clowns and Angels* I sent you on the 20th. In many ways, I believe that the new book on love, which I am finishing, to be called *The Clown's Grail*, will interest you more than those first clowns. But it means a great deal to me to know that you will look over the book and perhaps find things here and there which you like.

Strange that you mentioned Maritain in your last letter. I was talking with him the night before I received it and was asking him if he had read you. He hasn't — in fact, he has read almost no American writers — but I shall see to it that he does read you.

Over the Xmas holidays I read the first volume of your *Hamlet*. Tell me something about Michael Fraenkel. Who is he and where is he now? Your writing again, as it always has, left me breathless. There are so many perceptions which I feel immediately, so many new lines of thought, so many stimulations that I am played out at the end of a few pages!

If the project of 300 new *Capricorns* goes through, please have me put down for one copy. I can afford that, although I can't afford the new $50 book. But I have a rich friend who can, and who is a great admirer of yours, and I have sent him the circular letter you sent me.

The head of my department here at Yale — Henri Peyre — is an excellent critic — and thinks highly of your books. I have told him about our correspondence and your graciousness — and he may write to you.

The other day I was thinking how similarly you and [André] Gide affect me. I read both of you for a kind of nourishment I can get no where else. Although I often react against your ideas — but that is of no consequence — I react and draw in a new kind of life, a new way of living my life. I wish I could tell you how grateful I am to you for your art — and now also for your friendship and your encouragement.

Do you have a water color of a clown by any chance? How I wish I could see some of your pictures!

Here is the photograph of Rimbaud. May it give you some pleasure!

Goodbye for the present.

Yours,
Wallace Fowlie

1/6/44

Dear Wallace Fowlie —

Yes, only a few days ago, I received *Clowns and Angels*, and since then I have read most of it — feverishly. It excites me profoundly. I mean to write you at length about it — from Monterey. Until then I shall have neither peace nor leisure. I am struggling desperately to finish what work I have on hand before leaving. And even there I must continue to work. I loathe work! I long to recapture the luxurious feeling of indolence, of gayety and indifference I once knew. Now, despite all I do, I am besieged by people. I feel I ought to respond to every call, every demand — but in doing so I am unable to do what I really want to do — i.e. write the books and paint the pictures I have in mind. That is what the foolish struggle for "recognition" has brought about. I made a great mistake, perhaps. But I am learning fast. To know how to be most effective (just in the realm of "good") is one of the very great problems.

A day or two ago I sent you two photos, one of the only clown I ever made and the other of "a melancholy poet" (imaginary, of course). The latter someone bought already, and the clown some one has an option on. However, if you like the photos (I mean by this, that you may see nothing whatever in these painting efforts of mine) I will try to do another expressly for you — as a gift, to be sure. I seldom do anything twice — in fact, never. So, the second clown will probably be quite different from the first. So let me know your honest reaction. (Need I add that in my case the "color" is all? I am no draughtsman whatever.)

Frankel. Too much to give you in a letter. He lives in Mexico City — address Apartado Postal 181 — Mexico, D. F. I had intended before to suggest you send him some of your work — surely "Narcissus" and surely *Clowns and Angels*. Write him. He is Jewish, of course — from Polish Russia — Minsk, I think. Crazy about *Hamlet* — and all Shakespeare. Two of his books are worth looking up (you can try Gotham Book Mart,

N.Y.C.) — 1.) *Bastard Death.* 2.) *Werther's Younger Brother.*
The subject of Rimbaud fascinates him too. (I am going to
write you later about your words on Rimbaud, which I found
illuminating. The photograph came too! You know, I prefer
the rebellious ones — the "anarchist" expression. But this one
of the young boy haunts me, because it resembles a boyhood
friend of mine who later went to prison.) Please don't try to
buy any more of my books. Let me know what you lack, and
if they are obtainable, I will get them for you. I *am* indeed
interested to know that a professor at Yale should find my work
interesting. This never ceases to surprise me. Because, I say to
myself, if a professor really admired what I write, how could
he go on being the professor? I would destroy all institutions
of learning, if I could. Yet, when I read your books, I also think
to myself — how fortunate are your students in having you for
a teacher! So there it is, the little contradictions. But, you must
agree with me — these institutions (the bigger and better the
worse) are nothing but penal institutions of the mind. They
thwart more than they liberate. I got absolutely nothing (unless
poison and ennui) from school. I have learned everything on
my own, thru desire, thru enthusiasm, thru hunger. Can you
kindle *hunger* there at Yale? If so, bravo! Keep the doors open.
But I doubt it. I love the "guru." It's my pet image. Could I
be that I should account my experience on earth (this time
around) as worthwhile. But between the "guru" and the professor there is such a chasm, such an abyss, that words fail
me. I adore the Zen teachers too. And one of the three or four
I really venerate is Lao-tse.

Enuf! More again — soon as possible.

Two men you write about whom I never got to read — but
will yet — are [Paul] Claudel and [François] Mauriac. My
reading is so limited. Some men read *and* write. I find it difficult. I am somehow always surrounded by and plagued with
people. The worst ones are the admirers. Always I am fleeing —

seeking isolation. There must be something wrong with *me* that I don't achieve it.

I adore your clarity. All your phrases proceed, it seems to me, from deep meditation. You can say in a line some times what it takes me a chapter to say. I prefer *your* way. Silence! Silence! If I could only attain that!

Henry Miller

P.S. There are more people I want to make your work known to. I will suggest names as time goes on . . . And about my "ideas." How can one divorce the writing from the ideas? Isn't this like form and subject matter in painting? I wrestle with this in my work on D. H. Lawrence.

P.P.S. Only now am I getting back my copy of "View." Cannot buy any from "View" or any of the book shops. Too bad. I wanted to send your piece to at least a dozen friends here and abroad — to Cairo too — to my Greek friend, Seferis, the poet.

Same day — later

Since writing you this morning I received 6 copies of "View" from Gotham. The miracle! Today, while retyping material for the new book (*Sunday after the war*) ran across several things I thought you might like to have — all extra carbons — all apropos of things touched on in letters to you. Please excuse *terrible* carbon of "Of Art and the Future," but am particularly anxious to have you see this, even tho' I feel you will wonder at it and disagree with most of it.

Also enclose an announcement of A.N.'s [Anaïs Nin's] latest book. She is one of the people I thought you might like to communicate with. Also, here is another person for you — I have a rich correspondence with him: Claude Houghton, Esq. c/o Hughes Massie — 40 Fleet St. London, E.C.4.

Hastily,
Henry Miller

Anaïs Nin lives at 215 W. 13th St. NYC.

P.S. The "F" mentioned in my letter to Emil [White] is of course Michael Fraenkel. L. is [Walter] Lowenfels whose name you may know too.

1/19/44

Dear Wallace Fowlie —

Here's another chunk from the new book which I thought might interest you. No time for a letter now. Still haven't left for Monterey.

Wrote my London agents about your book — hope they may find you a publisher over there.

If you can dig up more copies of "Narcissus" for me, please do. I will buy any quantity. I enjoy sending it out all over the world.

In haste,
Henry Miller

Is the Yale Library going to take a copy of the "Angel," I wonder? Just received an interesting little book from London (one shilling) called "Henry Miller" — by Nicholas Moore. Gotham Book Mart, N.Y. is supposed to have 300 copies.

P.P.S. Have not heard yet from the professor at Yale — one of your friends.

Barbizon-Plaza Hotel
New York City
22 January 1944

Dear Henry Miller,

So many things to thank you for. First, the two photographs which I look at a great deal and which excite me. It would be wonderful to have an original clown from you, but your generosity embarrasses me. I don't deserve such a gift. But if you do one for me, I assure you that no work of yours will be more venerated!

I shall be at the Barbizon-Plaza for two or three weeks preparatory to leaving for London — so write to me there — although my mail sent to Yale will be forwarded.

I began the new work on Monday. It is a confusing world and I have many misgivings about this move. But if I am allowed to work up my own broadcasts, that will be sufficient freedom and I shall feel that I am doing something useful for France.

The passages on France in the manuscripts you sent me made me weep. I have felt all that, too, but am unable to express it as movingly as you do.

On all these pages which I have read and reread, I have found that strong dedication to art — that made me love you as a writer and as a man from the first time I read you. We meet on the *aesthetic*, and I believe we are one also in our apprehension of the tragedy of man, even if my explanation differs from yours. The important thing is that we feel and participate in the same aesthetic values and the same sense of tragedy.

I am sending you a copy of *The Chimera* (which is just out, although dated "Autumn 1943") with my piece on Hart Crane and Rimbaud.

I marvel at the strength of your writing, its conviction, the abundant fertility of your mind. You are an iconoclast, of course, in a sense, but you are also a lover. The tenderness with which you protect the things dearest to you explains the ferocity with which you castigate. At this moment in my existence when I am changing, temporarily, from the university to the O.W.I., your friendship is a kind of spiritual sustenance I needed. You are helping me over and I am grateful.

I wish I could write you a real letter, but I am sick with fever from a tetanus shot and more inclined to say, as you would put it, "fuck the universe" than try to inscribe my thoughts on paper.

May I keep the manuscripts you sent me — or do you want them back?

Yours as ever,
Wallace Fowlie

Jan. 29th 1944

My dear Wallace Fowlie —

From the moment you mentioned "the clown" idea, and then especially after reading your book, I felt that the painting belonged to you. So I managed to get it, by exchanging another for it, and I am mailing it out to you today — and very very happy about it. I only hope you won't be disappointed in it — sometimes the photos of my work look better than the paintings themselves. I am still a stutterer and stammerer in this realm. But if, as I believe, I have another twenty or thirty years, maybe more, to live, why there is hope that before I die I will achieve some mastery. I really wish to stop writing in another year or two and only paint — *and* write poetry. I wrote my first poems a couple of months ago. A wonderful experience. I want to end up as a poet, not only in words but in action.

You speak of your "explanations" being different from mine. Perhaps. But I find nothing to quarrel about in yours. I can accept everything you say. And, if you are a Catholic now, as I suppose you must be, that in no way disturbs me. You are catholic — with the small c. And that is what I would wish to be. I notice that all the deeply religious figures are in agreement, no matter what faith they espouse. To believe is to accept — I learn that over and over each day. I feel obliged to talk of these things now that you are going away. I imagine there have been questions in your mind — as to where I stand.

I have probably contradicted myself frequently in my writings. That doesn't matter, really. That is the sign of movement, of life, of experience the teacher. But I never regress. That is Satanic. (And in Hebrew it means exactly that, I was once told. Satan was a "back-bender." The "recidivist," so to speak.)

No, what is coming over me strongly these last few years — due to very definite reasons, due largely to certain meetings with other men — is the realization that the *décalage* between the writer and the man must be overcome. I have no respect for the artist, however great, who does not practice his art in living. Recently I observed with joy that I am able to act out my beliefs. One's behavior then becomes very simplified. All complications fall away. You have no fear of being either ridiculed *or* crucified. You have the deep joy of certitude. You know then, for the first time, so it seems to me, what the moral sphere really is. And, though you may disagree, I think the moral and the aesthetic are one. All is one. That's the utter, stark, simple beauty of it. I am now at a dangerous point because it is so clear to me that the right way is also the most advantageous one that I have to watch myself in order not to do the good, the true, the poetic thing *because I know it will bring a great reward.* In short I have that almost insane lucidity — like that of the criminal who knows just how and when to crack the safe — a lucidity about Heaven, if I may put it that way, and get to a point sometimes when I imagine I *could* open men's eyes. Only the knowledge that other, greater, far far greater souls were unable to do it (for the mass of mankind) gives me pause, and also a sense of self-criticism, a touch of saving humor too.

All that I am writing, in these books I feel I *must* finish, (a foolish conceit!) is behind or beneath this level I speak of. There is a schizoid quality here — of being one man and describing the other (the one I was). I sometimes think I ought to chuck it all. But then again I know that something of the present does creep into the writing about the past. I think, though, I lack the supreme courage here. I feel that the artist in me is getting the better of the man. This is *one* of my problems.

But that you — who take for your subjects the very men I adore — should be able to treat my work so sympathetically is one of the greatest incentives for me to continue. It means much more to me to win your approval than to win the praise of those who think and feel like me. One of my greatest tribulations is to meet the people who admire my work. I find usually I have almost nothing in common with them. Most people, so it would seem, like my work for the wrong reasons.

But enough of this. You make me want to confess to you. I sense so strongly your purity. I have only been honest. Not pure. And I am no longer proud of my honesty — it was too easy for me. I want to tackle the difficult things. I want to *earn* my freedom. Strange words from my lips — *earn*! Most things have come to me as gifts — they were not earned. I have been against earning all my life. And in one sense I was right. Perhaps I was made "rich" only that I might discover how poor I am in matters of the spirit. I am 52 now, but I feel as though I arrived at maturity only about six months ago. And that curiously enough corresponds to the moment when my ego was almost annihilated. I had been finding and losing myself. I believe now it is with me to stay. But again, if that were wholly true, perhaps I should not be using the pronoun "I." But at least now I know that "I AM THAT I AM."

Well, I shall probably write you again before you leave for London. I should like to send you away in a state of bliss.

One thing I regret — now that you are in N.Y. the one person in this world I should like to have presented to you is Anaïs Nin who lives at 215 West 13th St. I have the feeling that knowing her might be valuable to you — and to her too. I can't bring it about now — because there is an estrangement, not on my part, but on hers. She lost faith in me — and just at the moment (tho' she was unaware of it) when I was putting up the most heroic battle of my life, the moment when, had she been able to see thru the airs, she would have been proud of me. She was to me, and still is, the greatest person I have known — one who can truly be called a "devoted" soul. *I owe her everything.*

However, I have given you her address. You may, if you have the desire, find a way to meet her. I am sure you have friends in common, especially among the French refugees. Think of that! (I ought to tell you, perhaps, that she hates Catholicism — it poisoned her young life. But that does not make her irreligious. My friend [Conrad] Moricand in Paris always referred to her as "the perfect Neptunian." That should mean something to you, yourself strongly Neptunian, I suspect.)

There may be one very great favor I may ask of you before leaving N.Y. But of that I wish to think long before mentioning it. It concerns my daughter [Barbara] (now a woman of 24) whom I have not seen nor heard from since I deserted her and the mother some 17 or 18 years ago. Even here a strange and beautiful thing occurred recently. A woman her age came to interview me for *Collier's*. In the space of five minutes I learned she had met my daughter some two or three years ago (and apparently the girl did not *hate* me, as I believed she did). However — still a strange silence, an inexplicable one to me. I wait, and believe me, *I pray.* Rather than make a false move, I continue to wait. And so I will say no more — I have said more already than I intended. Maybe I have to do something which is very hard for me to do. I feel I am being tested.

Forgive all this — so much, so much. And all about myself. The ego killed? How patent it is that that is only another deception!

Every word in your essays *instructs* me, puts me more and more on the path. How religious all this sounds. And it *is*, I

hope. Surely we cannot be so far apart anywhere! Blessings
on you!

Henry Miller

Feb. 4th, 1944

Dear Wallace Fowlie,

I forgot to say in my last letter that the scripts I sent you
are for you to keep, certainly. Herewith I enclose a copy of
Quiet Days in Clichy (2 stories, mailing them separately —
registered) which some one is publishing for me privately
some time this year. I want very much to get this copy to my
old friend Alfred Perlès who is with the British army. He has
changed his name (or, it was changed for him by the army) to
Private A. J. Barret. His number is 13106734; he's in the Pioneer Corps. I cannot send it through the mail to England — I
am afraid it would be seized by the censor. Since the time I
wrote it I have been racking my brain to find a way to get it to
him. I wonder now if I dare to ask you to carry it to England?
If you feel it would cause you embarrassment or inconvenience,
please don't! In that case just leave it with my agents, Russell
and Volkening, 522 Fifth Avenue, N.Y.C. But if you can take
it to London, then please deliver it to J. M. Tambimuttu, Esq.,
editor of "Poetry – London," 26 Manchester Square, London,
W.1. Tell him I will arrange to have either Fred [Perlès] himself or one of his friends pick it up.

Incidently, Tambimuttu is one of the people whose names
I intended to give you anyway. He may be of use to you. He
is the first publisher in the Anglo-Saxon world (representing
Nicholson and Watson), who asks me to give him "everything." He knew Anaïs Nin and Durrell (Lawrence) and other
good friends of mine.

The others I thought you ought to meet are:

1. Claude Houghton — c/o Hughes Massie, 40 Fleet Street, London, E.C.4 (his home is at Mount Beacon House, Bath).

2. W. T. Symons — 15 Regent Park Terrace, London, N.W. 1.

3. Private A. J. Barret (alias Alfred Perlès, alias "Alf," alias "Fred"). We lived together a number of years in Paris. A strange fellow, Viennese originally.

Houghton, as you probably know, is the author of some strange books, such as *I Am Jonathan Scrivener* and *Julian Grant Loses His Way.* I have had quite a correspondence with him, but never met him. Hope to one day. You *ought* to have something in common with him.

Mr. Symons was the editor of a magazine whose name I forget now. I consider him the perfect example of a "gentleman," in the highest sense of that word. I have a profound respect for him. Since arriving in America I have neglected writing him, for which I am most ashamed. He symbolizes for me the best there is in the English character.

Chimera arrived, but I haven't had a chance to read yet. More anon.

Henry Miller

P.S. Since writing this my friend John Dudley has read *Chimera* and is crazy about it. He will write you. HM

Barbizon-Plaza, NYC
10 Feb. 1944

Dear Henry Miller,

How many things I want to say to you, and how many things I have to thank you for!

The painting of the clown reached me yesterday. I love it. It is here in my dingy room, the one object I want to look at. First, it is striking in itself and contains much I have thought about the clown, and then it is from you, by you, and has your signature.

Then today, *The World of Sex* came and I devoured it immediately and marked many of the passages I shall reread more carefully. It is an illuminating explanation of much of your work and your life. The book already seems indispensable for the piece I want to do on you one day.

The copy of *Quiet Days in Clichy* has not come yet. I hope nothing has happened to it. I shall be delighted to take it to Tambimuttu. Thank you for giving me his name.

The matters you refer to in your last letter — even in a veiled and somewhat hesitant way — greatly touched me. You have done me so much good, you have stirred me to work, to thought, to hope, — that I should like to be able to do something for you. Since the first note you wrote to me, I have not ceased praying for you — because I know that is how I can serve you best. You have a magnificent soul, one which is certainly loved by God. I feel that your greatest work lies ahead of you (you know how much I admire your work already completed) and it will be generated through a new kind of humility and love. I hope you won't be irritated by this. Yet I know you won't, because you believe in honesty. You are an example of honesty. That honesty, when fecundated by love of man and love of God, can produce perhaps the greatest work of our age. That is what I think of you, Henry Miller. I am a sinner. I am not "pure" as you say. But I would like to feel that some of the suffering I go through because of my sins, will help you, by means of the miraculous interchange of graces, to grow in the strength that is already yours.

I shall write to you again very soon. Tonight, I simply thank you for the clown.

Wallace

2/21/44

Dear Wallace Fowlie —

This is in haste, from Monterey, where I now shall stay awhile, chez Jean Varda. Where shall I address you when you leave America? I trust you will let me know. That you *pray* for me means everything to me. I think I have already felt the results. ("Grace" is a very big word to me!)

I am afraid this will reach you only after you have left N.Y. I will do nothing now about my daughter. This will have to find its own solution. It is a test, that's what I feel.

I find it practically impossible to pray. If I had God's power I would not change things by a hair. It is all divinely just. I do not know what to ask for in prayer, either for myself or for others. There *is* a divine order and when you begin to perceive it, sense it, you become quiet — especially about the ills of the world. More soon. Ever yours,

Henry Miller

Varda is a sort of artist-saint. It is a blessing just to be here.

Write me to Beverly Glen [West Los Angeles] as always. Mail will be forwarded. I may leave any time. For the nonce I am the *girouette*.*

(c/o Jean Varda)
320 Hawthorne St.,
New Monterey
Wednesday, March 1, 1944

Dear Wallace Fowlie,

Your letter of Feb. 20th only reached me today. I am not surprised at the change of affairs. I think you are being protected. You shouldn't ever question these changes from without; my experience is that they are always for our good. Later you will find out, believe me.

* Translation: Weathercock. — *Ed.*

To my surprise Heath wrote me recently that Robert Herring of "Life and Letters" had accepted my piece called "Of
Art and the Future" (most unsuitable for his staid magazine)
and would pay ten pounds *or more* (sic). There is a little
magazine called "Kingdom Come," edited by Stefan Schimanski and Henry Treece, also amenable. Schimanski is an ardent
admirer of my work and Treece detests me — flayed me in its
pages recently as I have never been attacked before. Curious
situation. So far, I must tell you, Tambimuttu has accepted
every writer I recommended to him. He edits "Poetry – London" on the side. And it is he who is arranging for an exhibition of my water colors in London.

And that is what occupies me for the time-being — painting.
I have to do fifty for him, a dozen or more for people who
ordered paintings, and some for the "Angel" book. And then
get a batch ready for the coming shows in Washington and
New York. Between times I am trying to finish the *Air-Conditioned Nightmare* to show Doubleday Doran. (I am still pay-
ing off the $500.00 they advanced me in 1940.) This finished
I resume work on *The Rosy Crucifixion.* The Lawrence book
I have put off until I find a haven of peace and quiet in a foreign land. I want to concentrate on it with all my faculties for
a year or two. It has been dangling now for six or seven years
— and I am glad of it, because as time goes on I get a better
perspective on it.

I must tell you I have to reread your piece in *Chimera* before saying anything about it. I read it in a bad moment before
leaving and was confused about it. Partly, I suppose, because
of the linking up of [Hart] Crane and Rimbaud. I can't read
Crane. I mean I don't find anything in him that others see.
My fault doubtless. But now here at Varda's I will reread it
one day and tell you my reactions. (My friend [John] Dudley, though, was crazy about it and said he would write you.
He is a most ardent admirer of your work. Almost a disciple.
And he is very critical, hostile to most men's work — though

without good reason. He's a Virgo. So is Man Ray, so is Varda, so is my friend Alfred Perlès, and that most charming Greek woman Melpo [Melpomene] Niarchos. So was Goethe! So there you are . . .)

I have been here a couple of weeks now and seen Big Sur. Hope to return there and go into retreat. Magnificent country, and entirely like [Robinson] Jeffers describes. Have met some very odd and very interesting characters. Especially a woman named Jeanne d'Orge, a painter in Carmel, whose work is entirely of the beyond. A strange evening at her house. Passed through the valley of death. At midnight suddenly everything lifted and I became jubilant and well, after almost passing out.

Varda is an extraordinarily interesting man. Last night he was talking about Tibet and Mt. Athos, promising me he would take me to Athos after the war. Had originally intended to become a monk, but refused to "sacrifice" his painting. And then I told him that were he now to retreat to a monastery it would be a sin — it would be like falling into the lap of luxury. Now, I said, you will have to be the monk in life, while painting — that is your role. He agreed. *En passant* he told me of Valentine Penrose, the English painter, who went to Tibet and has not been heard from since.

We talk of everything — in the evening, after we have washed the dishes. The place here is fantastic: an old barn, originally, which he made into a habitation. Everything here he made with his own hands. On the walls are his mosaics of cement and glass — all mythological poems, so to speak, with a curious Byzantine quality transposed into a modern key. I love to listen to him because he speaks a double language. He makes discourses which, if I were able to, I would love to put down immediately. Fifteen minutes later, when I go to make notes, I find they have dissolved. This is the kind of talk I love best. He is Greek, of course, and his long residence in France and England has given him a queer veneer. How long I stay will depend on my powers of endurance. The comforts are almost nil. I live in the midst of draughts and chills. Today I nearly dropped from exhaustion hauling big pieces of lumber, for the fire, from the beach. His wife lies in the big studio ill with jaundice. Strange visitors come and go — sailors, ranchers, farmers, psychopaths, monstrous females, erudites and scholars, society belles. It is all quite confusing. Yet despite it I manage to get some work done. And, of course, it is another experience.

Well, write me here until I notify you differently. You ask about the new book, *Sunday After the War*. That is due out in April. You will receive an announcement, I believe. I have an accumulation of mail to answer — something like 30 letters! More anon. I feel it is good you were detained here.

> Ever yours,
> Henry Miller

P.S. Did you get to see Anaïs Nin while you were in N.Y.?

> [from Monterey]
> Tuesday [March 7, 1944]

Dear Wallace Fowlie —

I was surprised to read that [Bern H.] Porter had asked you to write a chapter for a book about *me*. Had no knowledge such a book was being planned. He probably means to surprise me. I hope that the others he may have asked to contribute measure up to you! Yes, do ask all you wish. And do let me know if you lack any of the books.

Am just about to leave for Big Sur where I shall have a house free rent for a few weeks. Address me c/o Lynda Sargent — Big Sur, Calif.

> Hastily,
> Henry Miller

Wednesday
[March 15, 1944]

Dear Wallace Fowlie —

Believe I forgot to say, in answer to your queries, that you might just hold for me, until a later date, the mss. I sent you to take to London.

Am having the most wonderful discussions with my friend Varda. I feel now a little like those great Rosicrucians of the past must have felt when they went forth to meet their kith and kin. Maybe a new kind of voyaging is beginning for me.

Varda has put into my hands a little book he adores, called *Le Roman de Tristan et Yseult* (of Joseph Bédier). It is a supreme delight to read this. I had only a few days ago finished *Wuthering Heights* (for the first time). One of the most poorly written books I ever picked up. A feeble mutilation of the "double" theme. (How marvelous, by comparison is the *Dybbuk*!) It's hard for me to read English literature. I wish, though, I knew old English well, could read the language of the period when English was just emerging. By the way, do you by any chance have in your possession *Le Miroir Magique* of Pierre Mabille — and if so, could you, *would you*, dare lend it to me? I once had it in my hands and read it part thru. It fascinated me. More soon.

Henry Miller

Thinking of Porter's idea of a book about me by various men (I am not supposed to know, I guess) I am hoping he will be wise enough to include writers who detest me. I should hate to see a book come out in which there are nothing but eulogies. Maybe you can give him a hint to this effect. Maybe too *you* will touch on the defects, and perhaps the "evil" in me. Only a man like you could touch on these matters illuminatingly.

1248 Yale Station
16 March 1944

Dear Henry Miller,

Just over a few days many things have accumulated which I want to say.

I hope your friend Dudley writes to me. Could you tell me something about him? All that you said was that he is a "Virgo" and I must confess that I am not sure what characteristics you ascribe to that type. (Likewise, I am not sure what you mean by "Neptunian" which you called me!) I have no astrological knowledge and don't know where to acquire it.

I should also like to know something about B. H. Porter. By the way, I am very sorry to have let the cat out of the bag, by telling you of the proposed book. Of course, I had no idea that you were unaware of the project. Please don't betray me to Porter. I have a week's more work on a lecture I am preparing on Rimbaud to give in Montreal in April, but after that (next week) I hope to begin my essay on your work. I approach this with great fear because you mean much to me not only as artist but as friend. It is terrifying to write about one's friends.

No, I didn't see Anaïs Nin while I was in New York. I am not sure that I know anyone who knows her. I wish I had discovered some way to meet her.

Last night a few students were here at my place and during a conversation on the American cinema I read them some passages from your admirable essay on Raimu. The effect of your thoughts and your style is startling on young minds. You refresh and stimulate them after all the tedious hours of lecturing they have to go through. I am constantly getting testimonials from past and present students of the new life you give them.

Your clown's mask is now framed and hanging on my wall where it is admired by all who come here. I can't tell you how touched I am by all your generosity and your goodness.

I think of California now, for the first time in my life, because you are there.

Au revoir, cher ami. Votre main.

Wallace Fowlie

Am sorry not to own a copy of *Le Miroir Magique*. The Yale library doesn't have it either. I have just looked it up.

---

c/o Lynda Sargent
Big Sur, Calif.
[March 21, 1944]

Dear Wallace Fowlie —

Just a word to ask if you would send — *by American Express* — those (2) mss. I had asked you to take to England to Miss Janice Pelham — 52 West 52nd Street, N. Y. City.

I am here as a house guest until I find a shack to crawl into. Met Robinson Jeffers the other day. He has quite a wonderful place — the famous Tower, I mean.

Mail comes only twice a week. No phone, no radio, no newspapers. Monterey the nearest town for food supplies — 35 miles away. But the bloody visitors still manage to trek out here.

You can write me safely to above. Hope you are better adapted to the old life now. Am reading *Hebdomeros* by [Giorgio de] Chirico.

Just finished *Tristan et Yseult* (Joseph Bédier's arrangement). Last few days Hilaire Belloc's son was here. No Catholic, this man! Guess the father was a bad example. But I love his *Path to Rome*.

More anon.
Henry Miller

---

c/o Lynda Sargent
Big Sur, Calif.
March 24th 1944

Dear Wallace Fowlie,

Dudley — Virgo. The Neptunians . . . I'm afraid it would require pages to explain these symbols. If ever you meet Anaïs Nin you will understand the Neptunian thing. (Or Varda.) These two have amazing correspondences. However, about Dudley. He's a genius possibly — but for a year or more is living like a paralytic. Nothing wrong with him, except that he can't decide to make even the slightest move. Can sit on a chair all day, like a statue. He's a painter, primarily, but wrote one book still in manuscript which he will show to no one. I had glimpses of it — held it in my hand, turned the pages, etc. Written in a big ledger with a short blunt pencil, with a small hand, and many marginal notations. A colossal affair. His defect is his criticality, his inability to go out to others, his mania for perfection (Virgo traits). You are one of the few men whose work he admires. All that you wrote about Rimbaud, and again about Crane, moved him and terrified as well as enchanted him. (He sees himself as a sort of Rimbaud — though he's not so at all.) He has a marvelous idea for a magazine (which I won't go into — but it's unique, I can tell you) and I think he was going to ask you to contribute. But he won't write authors about it, or any one, until he's sure he can pay for contributions. And I imagine that just will never be. Incidentally, I find more and more men like him — young men, I mean, who have great talent, sometimes genius, but who are absolutely paralyzed. It's a disease. They don't commit suicide any more, as in the Wertherian days. They kill the mind, or the soul — a far worse thing. I never have known of an age where youth was so timid as today. How they dread the future! Somehow they do not seem to realize that the future always looks black — to every young generation. Or that there were [always] wars and revolutions.

As for Bern Porter . . . he's an up and going young man, a scientist, who came to me and asked for something to print, having a little extra money and a desire to do something worth while with it. He's undertaken to do a bibliography, an extraordinary one; asks me a thousand questions, and is now pursuing all my friends and acquaintances. But he performs! He's a veritable dynamo. You may trust him. No, I shan't tell him I know about the coming book. I wouldn't spoil his fun.

I marvel when you speak of preparing so painstakingly for a lecture on Rimbaud. I should think you could get up and speak without effort for a few hours. You give me the impression of being soaked in that subject. I wish I could be with you and hear the lecture. Years ago, in N.Y. I used to pay ten cents to hear John Cowper Powys lecture at the Labor Temple. That was before I had ever begun to write. I admired him tremendously. The other day I received a copy of *World Review* from England and in it is an article about myself, [Count Hermann] Keyserling and John Cowper Powys. I was quite bowled over, no less by the fact that Keyserling was one of the few eminent men of letters with whom I conducted an invaluable correspondence while in Paris. It never ceased to amaze me then that I enjoyed his esteem. And now here we are, the three of us, in an English review. Rather odd. By the way, if copies are made of your lecture in Montreal I would appreciate receiving one, yes? Rimbaud continues to fascinate me more than any other writer. I don't think the last word will ever be said of him. When he said somewhere: "Poet, creator . . . that man has never lived!" I jumped. I do so believe that. And he was the nearest to it, in my opinion, that ever walked the earth. He really took off. (Just as some day I do believe man will take off into the air, with his own wings.)

And now, quite inapropos, let me tell you — by way of contrasts — how much I was stirred the other night reading the closing pages of a book called "Foreign Devil" (not a good book at all) by Gordon Enders. The description of the Panchen Lama of Tibet, his aims, his ideals, his philosophy, is all so very close to me, so understandable. And I find nowhere in the Western World men with such an attitude towards life, or such coordination between ideas and action. It is that I admire in the holy men of the East. This emphasis on the correspondence between faith and action. This simple little matter is taking men tens of thousands of years to learn. And there can't be any advance, not the slightest, not a particle of an advance, until that becomes a fact.

If you go again to N.Y. just call Anaïs Nin up. If she's not in phone book ask Miss [Frances] Steloff of Gotham Book Mart for the number. Do you know Marcel Duchamp, Max Ernst, [André] Breton, [Yves] Tanguy, Leonora Carrington, Caresse Crosby . . . oh, I could think of lots of links for you. If only you could truthfully say you liked something she had written, that would be a sufficient excuse.

I had to smile when I read your words about California. I don't think it's a place for you. It is quite a desert. But I love the country itself, every phase of it. I may move to Carmel shortly. I have to move as the wind blows now. Wherever I have a chance to live most cheaply. I've been six weeks without a penny. It sounds incredible. But there are times when nothing avails. And I don't get disheartened easily. I am not now — simply perplexed a bit, irritated, annoyed. If I knew for certain I would never receive another penny I could adjust to that, but the devil of it is I may tomorrow receive a hundred or two hundred dollars. One thing I simply cannot get is regularity of income, even the most modest sort of stipend. This too must be a reflection of some inner state.

I am relying on the exhibition in London (when it comes) to bring me in a tidy little sum. I expect nothing here of my American friends. Well, I am going out for a walk now in the pitch blackness of Big Sur. We have skunks, coyotes, wild

cats and other creatures roving about. The Pacific is absolutely desolate looking — I can't get over it. The emptiest,
dreariest body of water imaginable. There must have been
more activity in the days when Mu was above the surface and
they came here from Easter Island.

Write me here till I advise otherwise.

Henry Miller

Have you heard of a Catholic writer named Erich Frank? I
enclose a card of Pantheon's to give you an idea of their list.
I have asked for the [Gustave Theodor] Fechner (naturally!).
He influenced the author [Algernon Blackwood] of *The Bright
Messenger* (one of my favorite books.)

---

address me thus hereafter —

Big Sur, Calif.
March 30th 1944

My dear Wallace Fowlie —

I think nothing can tell you better how much your writing
means to me than this letter addressed (but never sent, thank
God!) to a professor [Paul Weiss] at Bryn Mawr, who, by
the way, is a good friend of Erich Frank.

This will come to you via a friend in N.Y. who I wished
to have read the letter first because of its references to you.
Keep it then, as a little testimony of my great admiration.

Henry Miller

P.S. Does the *Yale Review* still exist? Do they pay for contributions? And do you think they would consider something
of mine? I have a few good pieces, ranging from 15 to 40
pages in length, which I am trying to place. The editors once
inquired of my agents *who* I was! No word from them since
— this over two years ago.

A little word — about your trepidation faced with writing about me. Have no fear, no concern. Indeed it is I who fear for you. If you espouse my work at all are you not in danger — both from church and college? Do you enjoy complete freedom? For me the great thing will be to see how you resolve or interpret the *superficial* conflicts in my character. You mentioned Gide once — certain analogies and affinities between us. I said in a review once that I admired his honesty — *but*, I have explained to you, I think, that this honesty is very little really. I don't like Gide's "deambulations" — if there is such a word. By 40 or 50 he should have known where the Path lay. He's a cross between a Protestant and a scientist — in their worst aspects. I can be dishonest, too, if I believe that being so I can do more good. Vision is the thing. The world of the spirit is too vast and deep for mere honesty to be of much value. And even commiseration I don't care too much for. What strikes me (once again) in the Tibetan and Hindu sages is their tremendous sense of reality — something unshakable, and as corrosive and devastating (for those who cannot bear the light) as nitro-glycerine. These men are rocks — but they know also how to melt down with love, as Vivekananda so well said. Dudley has never returned your copy of *Clowns and Angels*. I am ordering another, in order to write you more about it, about the good Catholic men you chose to write about.

You may hear from Kurt Wolff of the Pantheon Press — and other American editors and publishers. I am constantly bringing your work to their attention. If only I had been raised among men like Picasso, Claudel, Rouault and that great galaxy of wonderful figures in France! What pygmies all about me here in America!

1248 Yale Station
New Haven, Conn.
Thursday, 6 April 1944

Dear Henry Miller,

The mss. of *Quiet Days* are safely in the hands of Miss Pelham.

Yes, the *Yale Review* still exists. I believe it pays very generously. It is a one-man outfit, or rather a one-woman outfit. One woman is all powerful. I have sent her one or two essays which she has always returned, but I am going to ask Henri Peyre to speak to her about you. Peyre is the French professor here who admires your work very much, whom I mentioned to you, and who still intends to write to you. I am sure that you will hear one day from him, and, I hope, from the Review (although it is mysterious and unpredictable).

The letter to Paul Weiss is a strong piece which I am glad you didn't send to him. What you say in it about my little book touched me deeply.

Yesterday I sent off to Sheed and Ward the completed ms. of my new book, *The Clown's Grail*. This is the book on love which has been my work of the last two years, all my Yale period. It is my frankest book. Will it be accepted? It appears to me now too boldly psychological for Sheed and Ward and too Catholic for any other publisher! Now I am delivered, free of my child. And rather sick with my freedom. I have no more weight!

In the first awkward pages I have written about you (the essay for Bern Porter), many ideas have come to me which I want to deal with slowly and thoughtfully. However this piece turns out, I know it will only be a first attempt, a first statement, which I shall take up again to explore and develop. But I am now discovering one important thing: all the aspects of your art and your nature are unified. You are one person, one visionary. Your vision is multiple and changing and even contradictory. But that is as it should be. You are so right in your letters to me where, in little snatches, you describe yourself so accurately.

This Sunday is Easter. My thoughts will be with you, and my prayers for you. May you have a new resurgence and a new resurrection of the spirit!

Wallace Fowlie

Big Sur, Calif.
5/17/44

Dear Wallace Fowlie —

Just a little word to say that all your prayers for me are being answered. I am now in my new home, offered me practically rent free, have found a patron who offers to keep me for a year, and am soon to see here the young woman I have set my heart on — a romance by long distance correspondence. What more do I need? I seem to have everything I ardently desired. God bless you!

Had a very good letter from Henri Peyre recently.

How are you progressing with the piece you are writing for Porter? He knows now that I know. It was inevitable. (I don't like the title* he's chosen, do you?)

Have you seen Fechner's *Life After Death* issued by Pantheon Press, N.Y.? I hope so. Wonder how you like it. Some one is sending me [Georges] Bernanos' *Diary* [*of a Country Priest*].

Ever yours,
Henry Miller

---

* *The Happy Rock.* — *Ed.*

Big Sur, Calif.
June 5 [1944]

My dear Wallace Fowlie —

Enclose these letters just to give you a peep behind the scenes. Everything is working out quite marvelously. I'm now getting my work done, enjoy peace, and find myself surrounded by helpers of all kinds. The books are coming out too. Seven or eight are in the press — due out very soon. ([Ben] Abramson, of Argus Book Shop, is now bringing out "privately" a reprint of *Aller Retour New York.*)

So you see — *yes*! your prayers are answered. All prayers are answered. I bless you and send you my warmest greetings.

Henry Miller

Anaïs promises to start printing the *Diary* — *great news for me*! Thinks to do the first 20 vols. in one.

Big Sur
6/21/44

Dear Wallace Fowlie —

The book came and I of course immediately read your contribution — and the one on Nostradamus. Which reminds me — did you see my piece ("Of Art and the Future") in the March issue of *Life and Letters Today*, London?

You are the only man I know of, writing today, who understands the singular mystical relationship between the clown, the voyou, and the angel in man. When you touch this theme you make me delirious. More! More! I long so much to see the book on Love. It will be strange if, in this book of Porter's, you, as a Catholic, prove more liberal (as I think you will), more comprehending, more sympathetic, than the others. I am most curious (and not at all queasy about it) to see what you have written. I hope to write you more at length soon.

Things continue to improve. More help, more blessings. And more power to work. I work like a demon. (Against my very principles!) Am painting again (nights) and rolling up quite a collection — for London. I will see that you get a copy of the new edition of A.N.'s book shortly.

Your devoted friend —
Henry Miller

Is there any French publishing house in New York or Canada which is reprinting the good French books of these latter years? I long to get hold of a few favorites. What will they have when the enemy is driven off? *Ruins*. It's foul. What a quandary!

Yvan Goll (of *Hemispheres*) writes that some affluent French publisher, now in N.Y., wants some of my books for translation and publication after the war. But what filthy experience I had with French publishers — not one of the big firms being decent, honest, dependable — all crooks and traitors and skinflints — *and cowards too*!

How is Canada? Hopeless for *me*, I suppose.

HM

1248 Yale Station
8 July 1944

Dear Henry Miller,

Thanks to you, I know, I have just received the book of Anaïs Nin. I have begun reading it — with immense delight — and I shall write to her as soon as I finish — and to you, dear friend, also, about my impressions.

In Montreal, there is a small liberally minded Catholic publishing house (followers of Maritain) who are publishing some of the good books.

Editions de l'Arbre
60 ouest, rue Saint-Jacques

I spoke to them about you and your work when I was in Montreal this spring. Something may come of it. Why don't you write for their catalogue? So far the two young editors have put up a good fight against the reactionary powers of the clergy.

This good summer heat always turns my thoughts to France and to the vacations I used to spend there. Now we are beginning to see in the newspapers photographs of the French who have lived four years under German occupation. So many of those faces have traits of tracked and worried animals. I am afraid that everything in Europe will appear — and for a long time — old, useless, of a complexity which excludes any profoundness. Living in America is like taking a cure of rejuvenation. How well we have learned how to live healthily! How little we have learned to understand ourselves!

All the men today who are soldiers or exiles already participate in the struggle which will liberate human thought. Most of them are young. But we can count on youth. Truth is in the young. I feel this in every class I teach. How they teach me — these young students! How they succeed in reanimating my though which always seems on the point of becoming stabilized, morose, calm! How they are able to infuse in my thoughts all of their restlessness and questioning which fecundate me!

Your last letter made me happy.

> Devotedly,
> Wallace Fowlie

Big Sur, July 20th [1944]

My dear Wallace Fowlie,

Yesterday Bern Porter came and I had the opportunity to read your piece about me for his book. I was terribly pleased — because you wrote it exactly as I imagined you would. So glad you brought in the question of evil as you did, and also the obscenity. And finally God. Superb. I do hope you will be able to place it somewhere before it appears in book form. Do send a copy to England, because I feel quite sure Miss Ross will find a place for it easily.

And now, it appears, I am to write about you — for *Chimera* — a review of *Clowns and Angels* — which I am so happy to do.

One thing bothers me — that you received such a miserable pittance from Porter. It was unavoidable. He promises, however, that if the book sells, he will then make it up to you and to all the others too. Meanwhile, out of the fullness of my heart I wish to send you another water color.

Bern had the ms. of your novel with him. I asked him to let me read it. I hope you don't mind. I intend to sit down tonight and go through it.

And thank you for mentioning the Montreal publishers. I may write them one day. More very soon.

Henry Miller

Tell me, did you ever read *Julian Grant Loses His Way* by Claude Houghton, an English novelist? If not, would you let me send you a copy when I dig one up? I think it may mean something to you. I often wonder about your reaction to certain authors whose work I admire intensely.

I repeat — you are more tolerant, more liberal, more daring than all the so-called radicals. How wonderful to think that you as a Catholic dare to write as you do. Bernanos too, I notice. You are proving what it means to be a catholic spirit. Bravo and blessings on you.

There is one other book, most important, I bring to your attention — *William Blake's Circle of Destiny* by Milton O. Percival (Columbia Univ. Press).

Last night I had a very long session with George Leite, the youthful editor (21) of *Circle*; he is now living at Big Sur with his wife and child — in an ex-convict's shack. He wants something of you, preferably a chapter from *The Clown's Grail*, if possible. Now, my dear Wallace Fowlie, how can I urge you to give him this gift? He does not pay, but here is what I should like to do. Send him a chapter and I will pay you for it — $25.00, if that is not too small a sum. I am starting in tomorrow to make water colors — and will continue at it for a week or ten days. The boys will have theirs very soon, please tell them. This will bring me a little more money. Don't hesitate to accept. One should not give away such things. I can do it because I have no hopes of earning a just reward from my work — I am reconciled to it. But you mustn't fall into that attitude. Write Leite yourself, won't you — address Big Sur, Calif. (Anderson Creek). "Register" the manuscript, though.

We may meet before Paris. If I go to England, as I hope, I will come East. Then I will make a trip to New Haven. I want to meet you face to face. I want to see your room.

I don't know what I could have written [Jesse] Clark to have made him so happy. Young people always seem to fasten on me. I hardly know any men my own age. Moreover, I can't abide them. But I like very old ones — centenarians. They get young again after reaching a certain point. Become like amoral rocks. I am certain if we could live long enough — three or four hundred years — the whole moral problem would disappear. The spirit knows nothing of morals. Notice those who live forever!

I have a dog now, a young hound that wandered in to my place badly chewed up — perhaps by a mountain lion or a coyote. I adore him. Now I am teaching the two half-wild cats I have to be friends with him. I have wonderful moments with these creatures. They all follow me at night when I go for a walk. Sometimes, after midnight, I call the dog in and talk to him. This is a great moment indeed. He seems to go positively mad — chews me to bits. I put music on and try to make him listen. When I dance for him he gets panic-stricken. You should see him dive down a precipitous cliff. My heart is in my mouth. I have attempted to climb some of these walls of rock and had disastrous experiences. One arm is still out of commission. The whole terrain slips under your feet — you cling to a bush and it goes with you. It's terrifying. All decomposing granite — or greiss. The whole coast is a geologic fault. By the way, the dog's name is Pascal, of all things. He's a philosopher. Has ecstatic moments too, at 7:53 sharp — *le feu*! I think I have the faculty of hypnotizing these animals. Once I get my hands on them I can do anything with them.

The other day, going through my trunk, I ran across a manuscript on foolscap, fifteen pages, in hand, from my old friend Conrad Moricand, the astrologer and friend of Max Jacob. It is about the three mystic portals of Notre Dame and the cult of Isis. I wonder if you would care to read it? Rather esoteric, but it interested me enormously. He is a man I miss very much. (I miss few people in this life.) But he, Durrell, and Perlès I really miss; they meant a great deal in my life.

I have just finished reading Peter de Mendelssohn's *The Hours and the Centuries*, which my agent in England sent me as a gift. It leaves me utterly homesick for France. It is, I imagine, the country that [Jean] Giono writes about. I seem to recognize the woods and the high plateau which Giono treats of so lovingly in *Que ma joie demeure*. You know, this is one of my favorite books, as Giono is one of my favorite writers. I wonder what happened to him? I do not care if he became a collaborationist, Fascist, monarchist, traitor or what. I believe in him. He gave me great moments. I wish I could get to read Pierre-Jean Jouve. But above all, I wish I could lay my hands on that Pierre Mabille book — *Le Miroir du Merveilleux*. How difficult it always is to get the book one wants most! I am now advertising in magazines for certain books, offering water colors in exchange.

I have always such great good news from England about my work. It goes like wild-fire there. *Comme sur les roulettes* . . .

In *Fontaine* (Algiers) I read of Max Jacob's death. Quite a good article on him by Henri Hell. The episode of his conversion I particularly enjoyed reading about. Yet when in France I had difficulty reading him. But I know his paintings a

bit, and I've seen his letters to Moricand. Imagine, that he, poor
Max, used to send from the Monastery of Saint Benoît little
sums, such as twenty francs. M. used to say that it was probable
Max had stolen them for him. Quite. Perfectly reconcilable
with his character. Even in the monastery. *Et il tirait des horoscopes!* Why was he not in *Clowns and Angels*? Romain Rolland also died recently, I discover. And the author of *Alraune*
[Hans Heinz Ewers]. My June [Miller's second wife] was a sort
of Alraune. *

A phrase that repeats itself in my head — from your outline
— is: "the sun in Phèdre." I say it over and over. I am itching
to see what this imports. Also impatient to read the section on
Héloïse: human love. I could never get through the letters. Do
you really find them so wonderful? I wish I had been younger
and studied under you. Should I read Peyre's book? Sounds
overwhelming. I prefer little books. Though, God knows, I have
read some of the dullest and fattest ever written. (And there
was no dog Macaire in them to relieve the ennui.) . . . Now
they are bombarding here, from the sky. Have to stop. It's
deafening. Good night.

Henry Miller

Hate to stop. Go crazy here sometimes — never out of loneli-
ness — out of fulness! I open the half door and look out —
shout blessings to the world. Who hears, I wonder?

Big Sur
August 9th [1944]

Dear Wallace Fowlie,

I'm so glad you liked the second water color! Eventually I
hope to make a little collection for you.

---

* In Ewers' expressionistic novel of the twenties, Alraune is an extremely beautiful, but diabolically depraved creature who might well
illustrate the theologian Tertullian's argument that a woman's body
is "the antechamber of hell." — *Ed.*

I am sending herewith a carbon of the review I gave to *Chimera*. They wanted it short, they told me. If you like it, perhaps you can use it in dealing with the publishers about your other books. I shall also send a copy to Patience Ross in England — she may find a place for it in London. I hope you are getting on with her — she is very loyal, conscientious and not unintelligent, I find. Has done a great deal for me in a short time.

I am very much impressed with the table of contents for *The Clown's Grail*. Very. It seems to promise worlds. And I know you will fulfill this promise. (I am just reading *Maldoror* [by Lautréamont], in order to review it for *Accent*, and wondering what you mean by "the two monarchs.") As for publishers: first, I suggest Patience Ross, the agent in England. Then I suggest my friend John Woodburn of Harcourt, Brace and Co., N.Y. Then Kurt Wolff, the Pantheon Press, N.Y. Meanwhile my friend Bern Porter, who is here, seems excited by the outline, and wonders if he might do something, should the other big publishers fail you. I would reserve him for the last as he has not yet established much of a reading public. What about the Harvard University Press or the Princeton University Press? The latter brought out that most excellent book on Kierkegaard by Walter Lowrie which I reviewed enthusiastically for *The New Republic*. Please note the Pantheon's list of publications — there are a number of French Catholic writers on their list. He, Wolff, will bring out Léon Bloy soon. He published in Europe (Belgium, I believe) for ten or twelve years and returns when the war is over. This is all I can suggest for the moment. Later I may have more to offer.

Do you have a copy of the manuscript which I could read? I would love to see it. Please let me know.

I am just taking leave of the girl who came to live with me. It didn't pan out. We remain good friends, however. (Which means there was no passion in it.) This morning I made a rapid mental summary of all the failures of the heart I've met with — a shockingly big list. Yet nothing seems more important to me than love, unless it be truth . . . I also feel I shall be leaving here in another month or two. Where to I don't know yet. I wish it were Paris, Greece, Alexandria or India or China! My best to you!

Henry Miller

P.S. My patron has just shut me off too — unavoidably. Somehow I feel *better* as a result of these two disasters. More courage, more determination. Even joyous. Strange.

P.P.S. Since writing this I have retyped the review and sent it to *Chimera*; I also sent a carbon of the good typescript to Patience Ross. I send you the corrected pages because it may have a more special appeal to you. Perhaps too the students may enjoy seeing what happens to a manuscript in process. I am also writing Kurt Wolff and John Woodburn to advise them they may expect to hear from you.

Herewith a copy of my letter to Miss Ross, which please mail her a few days later, to make sure one or the other gets there.

HM

I had wanted to say in the review that I sometimes felt "the brush of angel wings" in your writing. But I say it to you. I wish I could immerse myself in all the books I long to read, now more than ever.

1248 Yale Station
19 August 1944

Dear Henry Miller,

So many things to thank you for!

The new water color has come back from the framer's and is now hanging in the place of honor. It is very striking and mysterious on the wall. I like to think of it as a spiritual portrait of myself, since you once called me "Neptunian."

I haven't yet had time to read *Life After Death*, but shall next week — and then write you my impressions. I am happy to have it.

Just this morning I received the extract from Perlès' homage. You *are* instrumental — and in many ways. Henri Peyre had already told me about the appearance of the essay in *Life and Letters Today*. I shall read it in the library next week. Peyre found it excellent: you have in Peyre a good defender and appreciator. I believe *Accent* is publishing my article on you in the next issue. This week I typed another copy of it and sent it to Patience Ross.

How can I thank you for the wonderful article on *Clowns and Angels*? Those four pages are the most generous and penetrating that have been written on my work. I shall try to live up to them in all future books. In the same mail there was a letter from André Gide who is pleased with the book and especially with the chapter on him: *Le miroir que vous me tendez sur moi m'explique beaucoup sur moi-même* . . . Your article and Gide's letter make up for the attacks. I feel invulnerable now.

I am reading, for the first time, and because of what you have written about it, Balzac's *Séraphita*. Have just begun it and shall continue with thoughts of you, of the supernatural and seraphic power you have over the rest of us . . .

                                 with devoted affection,
                                 Wallace Fowlie

                                 August 28th 1944
Dear Wallace Fowlie,

There are two men whose letters always excite me — you and Claude Houghton, the English novelist. Yesterday I heard from you both. Result: I have been writing you in my head all last night and this morning while going down the hill in a blue fog, a typical Blakean setting, with the sun *a pale blue*.

I also heard from [James] Laughlin [publisher of New Directions] at the same time. Here is what he writes about your ms., among other things: "I have Fowlie's ms. here now. It is extremely interesting, full of brilliant intuitions and judgments. If I have enough paper I'd like to do it. But I want to save my quota for regular authors such as yourself, [Kenneth] Patchen, etc. I don't think Fowlie would have any trouble in placing such an imposing work." I am going to write him and urge him to make room, even if he has to sacrifice me or Patchen. I feel certain this must be your very finest work thus far — no reason except that the titles of the chapters alone make interesting reading. (Even if you left blanks for the contents I would still think it a marvelous book!) As for Porter, I am quite certain he does not intend to publish it. It wouldn't have meant much to you if he had. Let me suggest another publisher I had overlooked the other day in writing you: Hardwick Mosely of Houghton, Mifflin and Co. — 432 Fourth Avenue, N.Y. Then there are also: The Creative Age Press (which just published Parker Tyler's book on Hollywood) and Macmillan. And what about Little Brown and Co. of Boston? They published [Louis-Ferdinand] Céline in translation — something I have never yet understood. I am sure Miss Ross will find an English publisher for you. (Though I am not so certain she will for the novel, if you sent her the script.) A propos of that novel — last night I was thinking — because of the liberation of Paris, which excited me to a fever pitch . . . I can hardly wait now to clear out! . . . I was thinking, I say, that your descriptions of that city were rather subdued. Then came this thought — that perhaps, just as you explained the religious attitude of Mauriac in his novels, your own feelings about Paris are so natural, so ingrained, so in the blood, that you cannot give us the shock of recognition. The character, by the way, who interested me the most, was the man of the church. I wish you had given more space to him. I always envy these figures! I wish I had time, in one lifetime, to also be a priest. For me it would be a luxury.

I wonder do you understand that? It is so easy for me (forgive this brashness) to live that kind of life: I mean to be good and to do good. As natural as breathing. And to think and philosophize within a rigid framework, how wonderful that must be! To rest within the bosom of the Church — ah, what a comfort! Really, you know, the grand problems of life only begin to unroll when you have dedicated yourself to the good life. It is only then that real doubt can assail you — the doubt, I mean, of action, "of doing good on earth" (the presumption of it!).

I wrote a review of *Maldoror* for *Accent*, which I doubt they will accept. I wish I had kept a copy to show you. I said in it that evil, real evil, is rare. (Later I thought of the war, and what people must think when they read such a line.) But I mean it. The war doesn't mean that evil is abroad. That is fear and ignorance largely. I don't even believe in the evil machinations of those German idiots. I know the Germans too well. Tender-hearted brutes — *pleurnicheurs*, as my friend Fred was fond of saying. How hard a Frenchman is by comparison! To get at his heart you need a pick-axe. When I read [Jean] Hélion's book (*They Shall Not Have Me*) I felt sorry for him that, having been privileged to be a prisoner of war, having endured that special sort of suffering, he had not emerged with some feeling for the good in the enemy. As I told him, the fact that he had at last discovered Goethe, learned to appreciate him in German, should have been worth the price of internment. Furthermore, I can never understand people who, when faced with an ineluctable situation, do not make the most of it. I would have had a good time with my captors, had they been German, Greek, Bulgar, or Croatian. But Hélion has no sense of humor.

You mention *Life and Letters* (Henri Peyre). Did you see my essay called "Of Art and the Future" in the March issue? And that stupid editorial accompanying it? That man Herring is really a herring, a red one too. In the Perlès issue he has a poem which is shockingly out of taste, something that makes me squirm and blush for him. Incidentally, my first poem in twenty years appeared in *Harper's Bazaar*, of all places, this August issue. "O Lake of Light" — you'll find it sandwiched in among the advertisements on page 4,937. (That was my farewell to Sevasty, the Greek girl, whom I loved madly.)

So, *Accent* is publishing your article on me! I will look for it. I feel sorry that you should have to appear in these little magazines. What a country this is! Not one good magazine for 140,000,000 souls.

I am curious what you'll think of the Fechner book [*Life After Death*]. I must tell you that *The Bright Messenger* of Algernon Blackwood made a profound impression on me. I believe he got his real inspiration from Fechner. I love this picture of the universe. It is one of life. Nothing but life. Life in the womb, life in the world, life in the beyond — but always life. It is strange how man accepted death before life. Interprets life through death. I think I've said this before, but let me say it again — the Bodhisattva is the greatest figure the human spirit has invented or conceived of. The Renouncer! How I adore that idea. I am one who hopes to be incarnated over and over again. This morning, coming up the hill in that blue fog, all so grandiose, so mysterious and eerie. I was thinking to myself — if in this existence I have life so marvelous, what of the next one, and the one thereafter? Even as animal I must have found it glorious. And as God — well, simply unthinkable. But in any stage — glorious . . . Must stop here to put up my loin of pork. More soon . . .

I count it a wonderful day when I first heard from you. One day I'll give you a song and dance about "Neptune" in your life.

Henry Miller

Big Sur, Calif.
9.21.44

My dear Wallace Fowlie, friend, mentor, guide, consoler, confessor and only man on this continent whom I feel really close to — your letter again, your moving words, always simple, swift, telling. Here I am answering it immediately, though it needs no answer. But this answering is simply response and response is love; you are the one person who gives me the freedom to be gratuitous, who leaves me room to write from impulse instead of duty. Why do I love Ramakrishna so much (rather than Jesus, rather than Buddha himself, even) — because he flung himself at God perpetually, an uninterrupted assault. This is the real *acte gratuit* that men like Gide and the Surrealists overlook. The only *acte gratuit*. Murder is all right — as literary ipecac, but murder is nothing compared to the ecstatic love of the divine . . .

What a strange thought, this! I had a four hour nap today and feel extraordinarily well as a result. The night is mine. I am all alone up here — not a soul for eight or ten miles around. The stars are out brilliantly. I have noticed some new constellations recently — and one fiery sun in the early evening sky. The Milky Way has shifted a bit, but is now brighter than ever, with a great rift in the middle, where new suns are being born, so they say. (What nonsense, all this astronomical lingo! What do they know? Almost nothing.)

There is a menagerie of bleeding stars . . . I started out thinking of Hugo's line. But I digress . . . I started out to ask if you would try to speed up the delivery of the text of *The Clown's Grail.* I have your outline of the contents before me. One I have put on the wall, by the sink, to study and dream over as I wash dishes or prepare a salad. My chores are endless, you know. It would amaze you. I am consuming myself. But flowing over. A full reservoir now. All I ask is a room somewhere, meals served to me, leisure to walk and think, a movie now and then of an evening, and — music. This I miss most — no albums of music. I have one record on two disques which I play over and over — it is about the death of Heredia y Varga, the bull-fighter, made in Mexico by a German company. I am saturated with it. I dance to it sometimes and shout like a bull.

Or I can weep too. I wish you knew that record. It is haunting. (From the Tonfilm *Carmen.*) There is one part called "Triana, Triana" — so moving. There is no music like this in our North America. No passion. We have no birds. (Only vultures and hawks. Here they abound. I come on them unexpectedly at times — eagles too — they scare the wits out of me.) Rattlesnakes too. At night when you step on a snake it gives you the creeps. To walk up this steep hill in pitch blackness is something to remember. There are things engraved on the rocks which you notice only at night. And the plants open and give out marvelous scents. But what blackness when the moon is hidden! The waste land par excellence. And in the morning fog and mist. Always, when I get to the top of the ridge, I am standing above the clouds — and there are aureoles and rainbows where they meet the sea, and the sky seems upside down, and clouds make cones and cathedrals, not just banks of floccus — or silkworms.

The following letter was written in my apartment at Trumbull College, Yale, where Henry Miller had spent two weeks. I had left early morning October 11 to teach and when I returned at noon, I found this letter on my desk. Henry had left that morning for New York.

mercredi — 10/11/44
(en quittant ma chambre)

Mon très cher ami Michel * —

Quelques mots en français d'abord. Dire que je suis comblé n'est rien. Je viens de lire vos souvenirs de France dans *Kenyon Review*. Encore une fois des larmes aux yeux. Vous allez croire

---

* "Michel" is a baptism name, used by some friends and especially French friends. Henry decided it was the right name for him to use. — *W.F.*

sans doute que je suis un "pleurnicheur," comme disait parfois mon ami Perlès à Clichy. Mais il y a des larmes et des larmes. Chez vous j'ai ajouté des sanglots. Vos écrits m'ont touché à l'endroit le plus vulnérable, au point où je me balance entre la vie élue, pour ainsi dire, et la vie choisie, peut-être vie destinée. Je suis d'accord avec vous plus que jamais. Si je l'ose dire c'est que j'ai vécu avec Dieu ces jours-ci. Les passages qui m'avaient fait pleurer étaient ceux qui m'ont traîné vers Dieu. Je vous absous de tout effort de me convertir (consciemment). Vous me séduisez, comme tous les grands esprits, c'est tout. Je ne serai jamais un converti — au moins je le crois — mais je resterai toujours un fidèle. Vous me donnez le courage de croire et d'aimer. S'ils viennent les heures pénibles pour vous, comptez sur moi. Je ferai place pour vous n'importe où je serai et je ferai votre défense contre tout le monde. Voici ma main amie —

Henry Miller

P.S. And now for other realities —

Don't overlook reading, if you have the time for it, these: *Dance Over Fire and Water* ([Élie] Faure), *Art and Artist* (Otto Rank), the short biography of Kierkegaard by the Princeton man (?). Ask [Janina] Martha Lepska (301 Prospect Street) to track down for you the book on the cult of the moon (Virgin material) by the woman analyst — or, if too vague, ask Anaïs Nin for the title. But Lepska has read a good deal on this subject, I learn.

When you speak of [Gérard de] Nerval (*Aurélia*), are you referring to "Life and Dreams"? (Had a profound effect on me — just when I lost Sevasty, the Greek girl.)

Why do you call Kierkegaard thinker and not "theologian" too? (admitting he fought them — but like Abélard again.) Can one say in English "a religious"? (or is this from the French?)

Have you mailed copy of *Clown's Grail* to Patience Ross? (I will write her about it anyway — *glowingly*.) Count on me to get it published!

Le Cimetière Marin ([Paul] Valéry) — have always wanted to read it. Is it truly extraordinary?

Am much moved by two references to Nerval —

1. Si je meurs, c'est que tout va mourir — and

2. Your saying he had no real desire to live. (That I knew as a boy of 8 and again at 16. *But* — it explains also why I *have lived so much*!) Do you understand? In reality I wanted, like Plotinus, to live the ineffable state — to skip this terrene condition. Alors j'ai fait le compromis. J'ai descendu et j'étais descendu! Hence the terrific impact (written into that water color) of Rimbaud's — *moi, je suis rendu au sol, moi qui me disais mage*, etc.

I could write on endlessly. Time is short. Will resume from elsewhere. I'll continue to write you from the beyond.

Et enfin — et plus gravement . . . I may take Lepska with me to California. It's come to that already. Here I put my whole trust and confidence in you. I wish her no harm. I want to open new worlds for her. *But*, should you feel I am doing her an injury, I give you permission to dissuade her — in the name of God.

H.M.

Oct. 30th 1944

Dear Michel —

Yesterday by great good fortune I received as a gift from Paul Radin, the anthropologist, the collected works of Rimbaud. Read immediately Claudel's preface, which I had never seen. Curious coincidence — I opened my study of R. with the same citation he uses in the beginning — on "being awake." Everything he said in that brief preface was as if already thought out by myself. I was in a trance. Then I *am* on the right track! What else did Claudel write on R., can you tell me? I'm using three librarians (good ones, too) out here but no books forthcoming, no hints, clues, suggestions. Last night I attended a class in the Labor College where George Leite lectures on Art and Lit. Spoke on Dadaism. What a strange sensation I had. As if transported to another planet. What meaning can such a subject have for these Californians? If there was once a bridge between the old and new worlds, it now seems gone. The whole farce and futility of education (*cultural* education) in America suddenly appeared in the grisly light of reality. I tell you, the reality of this moment is that the whole shooting match is about to be extinguished. What I realized (with blinding clarity) as I sat there, was that the poets prefigured the end long ago. We are simply going thru the motions, life [*sic*] sleep-walkers. As Krishna said to Arjuna — "the battle is already won!" And I say to myself — "All you wretches are already dead and buried." (And a lone voice pops up towards the end with a question — "Are the coming writers *religious* perhaps? Is there an apocalyptic school?")

Well, tell me if you have anything on R. by Claudel, by [Paterne] Berrichon, by Isabelle Rimbaud, the sister. Strange, strange, that I, not a devout Catholic, said exactly what Claudel did — that what matter if it took 37 years of anguish for him to see the light, and accept the truth? God, if I had only met some men of stature earlier in my life!

[postcard]
Fredericksburg, Va.
11/27/44

Dear Michel —

Lepska and I are getting married here in a day or two. We want your blessing on it. The address is 806 Hanover St. c/o

Raleigh Drake. All good thoughts for you. I feel I am doing right.

Henry Miller

Fredericksburg, Va.
12/6/44

Dear Michel —

Yes, it's difficult now to focus on external things. I'll probably write you from Boulder, where I'll spend a week or ten days. Lepska told me you were ill. But I assume that by now you've recovered.

Do let me know what happens with each publisher — and don't be discouraged too easily. It's always thus. I wanted to tell you that *Modern Reading* (England) is an anthology put out once or twice a year, I believe, by Reginald Moore — it's supposed to be good — *solid*. And you'll probably receive eight guineas or so for it. Incidentally, have you thought to offer it to one of the French revues for translation? I think it would be accepted.

I hope the show is a mild success. Too bad I wasn't able to muster more of the better water colors. I do hope that Harvey Buchanan is reliable and will get back to me eventually some of the more precious items.

We are still waiting for papers before going thru with the marriage ceremony. Lepska joins me in sending our warmest greetings.

We'll be in Washington this weekend chez Caresse Crosby.

Keep well! And remember me to Henri Peyre please. The more I think of him the better I like him.

Henry Miller

[card from Lepska]
Fredericksburg, Va.
12/7/44

Dear, dear Michel — We think often of you here — and your warm blessings. In some rich, strange fashion you have become a closer bond between us. We learned to love you together. How one can talk in the South! This wonderful slowing of the pace here is intoxicating — one feels in the possession of powers to do anything — unlimited freedom to live and love. *Nous t'embrassons bien tendrement.*

Lepska

How goes the Millerana — and your jungle fever? Friends should live together — and not in this abysmal inaccessibility. We miss hearing from you.

Wednesday — 19th Dec. 44

Dear Michel —

I'm only too glad to give your friend [David] Sudarsky what he wants. Sending him care of you a water color and a pen and ink self-portrait. If this isn't enough (I had no other w.c. on hand) I will send another water color soon as I can get round to it.

We haven't yet moved into the shack below. I work at my "studio" nearby however — an 8 mile walk each day.

I'm going to write you soon about Christ's life after the resurrection!!! Have suddenly seen a great light — from this phase of his life. Do you know any good work written about this significant phase of his life? I had written about Rimbaud in this way — and then wondered.

Am more than ever burdened. I seem to have a million connections with the world. I am heartily sick of it.

Henry

(The enclosed Xmas greeting was done by an admirer for himself.)

[card]
Boulder, Colo.
12/20/44

Dear Michel — We finally got officially married three days ago in Denver. This is quite a marvelous spot — grandiose scenery and weather soft as a duck's back. Merry Xmas to you from Lepska and self. Hope you are well.

Henry Miller

[from Boulder, Colo.]
1/8/45

My dear Michel —

Your letter has just come and I hasten to reply. You sound low — the saddest letter you've ever written me. And such solemn news about our good friend Jesse Clark! I wrote him at once and will continue to later.

I of course am feeling so wonderful it's hard to put myself in others' boots. Everywhere the news is sad and calamitous — most ominous. But I continue to believe, out of some instinctive certitude, that the war is nearing its end — despite all appearances.

That you are able to think about your work — new books too — is a good sign. You are suffering from exhaustion — not physical, but neural. I feel you should *not* be in a college — but in some peaceful, harmonious retreat. How can one write such books as you write *and* teach *and* interview all those young people? It's beyond human endurance.

We are still here, as you see, but hope to leave for Salt

Lake and San Francisco in a day or two. Everywhere we receive messages of good will, invitations to come and stay a while. This, in a way, is my reward for writing the books. Friends, new ones, spring up like flowers. I long, however, to be back in the cabin at Big Sur with Lepska. I feel a wonderful new period opening up. Also — a great change in my style, to the joyous, the imaginative, the world of dream and truth and reality, in the best sense. I long to "dispatch" that program I laid out and get on to the new level — the "open" level, I'd call it. I'm sick of dragging my old (unreal) carcass around, in novels.

Well, more anon. This is just a quick response to lighten the pulse beat. Love from Lepska who is joyous. She will write separately. And always best of greetings to Henri Peyre. Ever yours,

Henry Miller

P.S. More and more I want to read that Mario Praz book [*The Romantic Agony*]. Here I found *Steppenwolf* (Hermann Hesse) and reread it with great joy. Also [G.K.] Chesterton's *St. Francis*!!! St. Francis lifts me more than Christ himself.

P.P.S. It may sound simply ecstatic but more and more I want only to lead "the good life," to act out the simple teachings. I hug my poverty, my trust in others, my great peace. This is the climacteric.

1248 Yale Station
25 Jan. 1945

Dear Henry,

Your letter quickened the pulse beat. Believe me, your faith in the future means a great deal to me at this moment when matters of personal import for me have been somber.

On Tuesday we gave the performance of French scenes I

have been rehearsing for some time. They were well received. We gave a Villon poem, a Rimbaud poem (recited and danced), a scene from Molière, and a scene from [Jean] Cocteau's *Antigone.*

Perhaps you have heard how active Cocteau has been these last four years in Paris. He has scripted two new films: *Le Baron Fantôme* and *L'Eternel Retour*, and he has written and produced three new plays: (1) a farce-parody *La Machine à écrire*; (2) *Renaud et Armide*, called the most beautiful play presented at the Comédie-Française during the German occupation; (3) a new version of *Antigone* with music by [Arthur] Honegger. The scene we put on from his earlier *Antigone* has convinced me, all over again, that Cocteau is one of the great writers for the French theater.

Reports about Jess Clark continue to be bad. He has lost fifty pounds and is now suffering continuously. His face looks like a martyr's. My visits with him at the hospital are among the hardest experiences I have gone through. Two Sundays ago, the Gospel read at mass helped me: it was Christ's first miracle — the changing of the water into wine at the marriage feast of Cana. That seemed to apply so directly to Jess.

A request has come from England to do a new essay on Gide for a new critical volume on contemporary writers. The idea pleased me and I have started work on it.

I like to believe that you and Lepska have reached Big Sur, and that you have begun some of the new writing. How that announcement thrilled me! Everything that has come from your pen, that will come from your pen, is precious to me. You assert and justify so many of the things I believe. My love to you and Lepska.

Michel

Big Sur   2/9/45

Dear Michel,

First of all I want to quote from Lawrence Durrell's recent letter from Alexandria: "I am half-cracked with pleasure and am reading Pierre, the Fowlie (*Clowns and Angels*, I presume), and everything else simultaneously. It is wonderful to get bright gleaming books and periodicals. They all arrived simultaneously and I find the Fowlie absolutely marvelous in its purity and acuteness. It's so rarely a critic can write about the *experience* that made a work of art as against the critical aspects of the work itself; the last chapters are very profound and written with such clean lines. Is it well known at all, this book?"

Durrell's address is c/o Publicity Sections, British Embassy, One rue Toussoum, Alexandria, Egypt. He is connected with some little review there, or in Cairo, and would probably be glad to write about you. I am urging him to do so in my letter, and also warning him of the *Clown's Grail* and the *Rimbaud* to follow.

The other day I had a letter from Lawrence Clark Powell, librarian at U.C.L.A., telling me his former friend at the University in Dijon (where I met Powell) has started a Franco-American review in Dijon. His name is Georges Connes, I believe. He says they are in urgent need of American contributors. Their first number included Valéry and Mauriac. I wrote Powell to get in touch with you for material.

I am trying to get hold of an extra copy of a brochure called *Foundations Unearthed*, by Maria Bauer of Glendale, Calif. on the Bacon-Shakespeare controversy and its repercussions in Williamsburg, Va. It made a tremendous effect upon me on rereading it. Copies are scarce. Don't jump to any conclusions until you read it. If possible, look it up in the Yale library meanwhile. You will be dumbfounded, I assure you.

Everything goes wonderfully here. The weather is superb. Golden days and lush green hills. It's warm. Lepska is in love with the place. I myself love it more and more every day. I wish you could come out and see it for yourself. We would find a way to put you up comfortably if you did come out . . . Meanwhile my best to Henri Peyre. I wrote Jess Clark the other day again. More soon.

Henry Miller

P.S. I'm now getting ready to do a portrait, for "The Nightmare" of that great Negro preacher in Chicago, who talks of "Jesus! The Light of the World!"

February 19th, 1945

My dear Michel —

Lepska has gone into Monterey to send you a wire. I can't tell you how bad I feel for you. I of course expected no miracle — and I hope this doesn't sound cruel. From the moment I heard the terrible news I realized that it was his destiny to meet such an end. Why, I can't explain. That he suffered such tortures, though, is agonizing to hear. Why this must be for some — especially those who do not merit it — is one of the greatest mysteries we have to contend with. I remember Dostoievski speaking about his faith in God but not being able to understand why children — who are innocent — He permits to be tortured.

I want you to know, too, that I did think of Jess Clark frequently and that some weeks ago I urged Bern Porter to send that second water color to him, saying expressly that "Clark was dying." I understand he has sent it — but too late, as you say. Whether he sent it to the hospital or the Yale address I am not sure. I know I gave him the hospital address. That water color is a very strange one — one I myself don't understand. Perhaps you will make something of it. It *must* mean something!

I hope you will forgive me for mentioning this now in the same breath — it is about my Red Notebook, which I loaned [Harvey] Buchanan for the exhibit. He seems not to be able to find it — according to my friend [Richard Galen] Osborn who heard from him. I fear it has been stolen by one of the students. I am not surprised, neither am I angry. It happens though that I need it — for reference. It is the only record I have of the "journey." Furthermore I had offered it to Porter as a gift. And beyond that, it was to be printed by facsimile process. Now I wonder if in some subtle way these facts could not be spread abroad on the campus. Perhaps the man who has it would then return it — under a pseudonym. I in turn will promise him an autographed copy of the facsimile copy when it comes out. He needn't reveal his identity to anyone but me — I shall safeguard it, on my honor. I would have offered to return him the copy he has taken except that it is a gift to Porter. Maybe if he knew my feelings he would act. If not, *tant pis*.

To revert to your loss. Strange that the other night, whilst reading *Death and the Lover* by Hermann Hesse I should think of you and Jess Clark. I don't know whether you would suffer afresh by reading this book now. I have only read about fifty pages — but I am deeply touched. It is about a young teacher and his pupil — in the Middle Ages, in a monastery. The theme is beautiful. And one very close to you — *to all of us*. In this book there is a biographical account of the author, which again will interest you. Perhaps me even more.

It is exasperating to hear that *The Clown's Grail* has been rejected again. It makes me furious. More than any of your books I value that one. I tell you, if they all reject it, I will have it printed at my own expense — *selfishly*, because *I need it*! I can never express what it meant to me to read it. But let us keep trying meanwhile. I do want to know what my English agent has said about it. I feel certain that if I wrote to six prominent English publishers with tears in my eyes —

and the bait of letting me pay for printing, or else guaranteeing its sale, thru my royalties — they would take it. I cannot believe the English will be so blind — as us. Let *me* pray this time!

Don't despair! You won't be overlooked. If a sinner and a renegade like myself can feel the importance of your work — *the healing power* — then others will too. It is because it *is* so meaningful that it is being ignored. This is a period of closing the eyes to what is of vital importance. Now that I am being accepted more and more readily, I begin to realize that I could not have been as strong, as deep, as sincere as I imagined. It was a sign of weakness to expect to be accepted in one's own time. I dislike my readers heartily — most of them. I have nothing in common with them.

More soon. I am burdened with work, really.

Henry Miller

In the current issue of *Tricolor* you will find my article on obscenity — which I wrote with great effort. The last third of it seems important to me. I don't think anyone has written in like manner on such a subject.

1248 Yale Station
8 March 1945

My dear Henry,

I am sorry to report that THE LITTLE BOOK (*das Büchlein*) isn't in the Yale library. When I see Mr. Bluhm, the Luther specialist, I shall ask him about it and if it is possible to procure it.

I can't tell you how upset I am about *The Red Notebook*. I knew nothing about its disappearance. Harvey Buchanan has left New Haven and will soon be sailing for France to work with the Quakers there, but last evening I gathered several students who had attended the exhibit and told them about your *Notebook* and about your generous offer. Let us hope that word reaches the ears of the offender and that reparation will be made!

My teaching this semester is very light. I am resting, deliberately, a part of each day, and working very slowly on the new pieces. Then I turn in about ten o'clock at night. I am bored with myself but I know that I have to go through a few months of this régime in order to get back my strength and my equilibrium.

Suffering — bodily suffering — is a great privilege. We lose courage so easily. Nothing is the same after suffering. There is a new shadow on everything, a new depth in our words and in the color of the sky. How foolish it is to try to resist suffering. What insignificant wretches we make ourselves into by not sitting still in the center of the suffering and uncovering our eyes. We have to learn how to go with suffering as with a great tidal wave that will take us toward a new world.

I think of you and Lepska as in a land of sun and happiness and love, and I can't tell you how much good that thought does me.

                                        Michel

————————————

                              March 19, 1945

Dear Michel,

It interests me much to learn that several chapters of *The Clown's Grail* were first written in French. You remember, when I first read you, I had the impression French was your mother tongue? How I envy you this gift!

I sent you four of [Raymond] Queneau's books yesterday. *View* ([Charles] Henri Ford) has the other two, two of the more recent ones. I read two or three of those I sent you while in France. He's hard sledding for me. Yet, if you could do something about showing them to an American publisher I would appreciate it. I hate to think of you reading them all. Maybe Peyre and others would share the burden? If you would like to see the ones *View* is reviewing please write Ford to send them to you — at my request.

I'm glad you are not going to teach this summer. It's obvious you need a rest. And I wish I could go to Montreal with you — I was there only once — and liked it. That was before I knew a word of French. There I saw for the first time the words — *pompe funèbre* — they fascinated me.

It's also good that you are not called this or that. That means you cannot be pigeon-holed. I think you could manage to live and write without teaching — if you really wanted to. Your fears amaze me. You know, where faith is strong fear cannot enter. You have faith in God — but how about faith in yourself? Maybe you have yet to make full surrender. These worries are not yours . . . it is the world creeping in. The world is sick and poisoned today. I don't think there could ever have been an age of less faith. And it is this which is killing us. Put yourself completely in God's hands — He never worries.

I finished a marvelous chapter of [Franz] Werfel's last book [*Star of the Unborn*] last night and went to bed dancing. It was about angels. I think it would bore you to read such a book — I go on because I can't resist it — but glance at table of contents and select spots, if you care to. The chapter on the High Floater, in which Werfel discovers "what was the most important moment in his life" may mean something to you. The angels appeared during the trip to Jupiter. However cheap the style, something seeps through . . . the man over-reached himself. And at least we get God, creation, angels, spirit, etc. It's a rum book. I can't drop it, though he irritates me continually.

But [C.F.] Ramuz' *Présence de la Mort* was marvelous —

particularly his ending. Soon I will come now to Léon Bloy.

I never cease thinking of you!

Henry

Cable from Paris today says 300,000 frs. on the way! I earned almost 2,000,000. Imagine that!

April 11th (eve of the
new moon), 1945

Dear Michel —

I am in the middle of a long discourse on Villon in Francis Carco's *Nostalgie de Paris* and I am filled with emotion, a sort of anguish which I can't define. Carco is a writer, I must tell you, who speaks to me as only a few of my favorites (and they are not "the great ones") do, or know how. This word *nostalgie* — I feel this in every book of his I pick up. Now comes this one, which I have been reading slowly, only between times, because I have so many books to read and so much to write too. But what a reward. I thought you ought to know of this little book of Carco's, published at Genève, 1942 (Editions du Milieu du Monde). I remember vividly your words about Villon. This exegesis, so to speak, rounds out yours. Carco is very human — maybe "sentimental" in the eyes of the French. I don't know. But he *warms* me.

I had to weep several times in the reading, about Villon. (Same as when I read his Utrillo.) I am in the "open street" again, with him, and all that he relates of the bad side of Villon touches me deeply. It is almost like reading about myself. But what affects me most, what really rends me, is that my inadequate knowledge of old French deprives me of the joy of tasting him to the full. Carco's own idiom is rich, a curious mixture of the academician and the master of argot. Wonderful fat croaking gutter words he deploys — so redolent of the terrene French! I am walking the streets with him

— the streets of Paris. He mentions the rue Grégoire-de-Tours. Here Brassai, the photographer, used to repair on rainy days to a certain whorehouse where he played cards with the Madame.

But Villon . . . Read what Carco says of the "poet"! You will enjoy it. Certain passages should make you jump and quiver. What a panegyric! I wish I knew where Carco were now — I'd write him or cable him.

I am obliged to read some fifteen or more war books, to review for *Town and Country*. To read Carco is like taking a day off. How I loathe English language books in the main. One page of French and I am set up, my day blest. How I wish I could get more French books! I need them. The others depress me. I feel that the language has been exhausted.

After citing the following two lines, Carco says (and how my heart leaps!) —

> Mort, j'appelle de ta rigueur,
> Qui m'as ma maistresse ravie . . .

Carco: — "C'est par de pareils mouvements qu'un artiste — si bas qu'il soit tombé — commande l'admiration. Songez qu'il y a près de cinq siècles que son oeuvre fut écrite et qu'elle n'a pas une ride, qu'elle est vivante, humaine et pleine de sève comme au premier jour, et qu'après nous elle continuera de réconforter, d'éblouir d'autres hommes. Je m'adresse à ces hommes qui viendront et découvriront à leur tour chez Villon cet élan d'âme et de coeur qui nous a si profondément émus, et je les mets en garde contre la légende dont on a entouré ce poète. Qu'ils reprennent le *Testament* et cherchent dans ses huitains et ses ballades, moins l'explication d'une époque que celle de l'auteur. Ils verront combien Villon est grand au milieu de sa misère et de sa souffrance, comme il a fallu qu'il fût — par sa faute — abandonné de tous pour qu'il poussât vers le ciel sa clameur désolée. Le reste importe moins. Ce n'est que lui qui compte et, quand, après cette crise,

il poursuit la distribution de ses biens et l'accompagne
de railleries, d'équivoques, d'allusions, son naturel est si
plaisant qu'encore une fois il nous ravit."

Tonight I feel desperate about my separation from Europe.
Anywhere over there would have been better than here. Even
among the Turks. The monotony and sterility of our tongue
afflicts me like a poison. Monotony of, or rather absence of,
spiritual, moral, cultural, sensual values. I am deeper in the
desert than ever Augustine was. God, when I get to that section of the "Nightmare" (*Remember to Remember*) which is
about France, I'll crack the gates asunder. I'll drown this desert of a land with beauty and tenderness, with nostalgia for
"a land unknown." For vol. *three* I have the germ of a brilliant idea — the depiction of the Utopia America has dreamed
of becoming (and may well become thousands of years hence).
The [Maria Bauer] booklet on Bacon (*Foundations Unearthed*)
planted a seed in me. Maybe that whole gang — "the Shakespeare Group," as they were called — had a vision of the
Promised Land in the midst of the terrifying violence of the
Renaissance. Maybe there is something much greater behind
this mystery (of the plays) than anyone now suspects. I am
going to follow my hunch.

Well, enough! I must continue reading my "assignment."
Quelle corvée! Now wading thru [Arthur] Koestler's *Arrival
and Departure*. He's the martyr type, but without benefit of a
Paradise here or beyond. The more the war draws to an end,
the worse the situation looks. From outside anyway — maybe
not within the maelstrom.

Henry

P.S. Had a good letter from Anaïs Nin recently. Quite recon-
ciled now. She spoke highly of you and your work. Only worried about your Catholicism (in the work). Sic! Like saying
the cathedral is excellent but don't like the corner stone. She
will come round yet — she must.

[card]
Easter Sunday
[Apr. 15, '45]

Lepska, the dear girl, went to the woods early this morning (while I was snoring blissfully) and knelt down on the pine needles to pray for us all. I felt like a real sinner when she came back and told me. But somehow I can't to the woods any more — for praying. However, as I finished *Death and the Lover* the other night I thought of you — it was a kind of prayer, I guess — "to all and sundry," as Alf says. Would you like me to send it to you?

Henry

[card]
4/18/45

Dear Michel,

Yes, I did get everything and thank you for the montage. I'll try to get it back to you later, if you like it. Porter got back (undelivered) the water color for Jesse Clark. I've asked to have it so that I may be sure *you* get it. I'm sending the Hesse book today. Deep in work. Joyous now. Slaving betimes on the Rimbaud translation. Caresse is writing you! She's a good person. I recommended something from *Clown's Grail*. Forgive this quick scratch.

Henry

1248 Yale Station
25 April 1945

Dear Henry,

Your last letter sent me rushing to Carco. I read *Nostalgie de Paris* and reread some of the novels: *Les Innocents, Per-*

versité, Jésus-la-Caille. I don't feel as strongly about him as
you do. His sentimentality gets monotonous.

But your letter turned my thoughts to Paris and to all the
deep nostalgia I feel for it (as you do) and which I try to
submerge daily. I think of Paris as the one place, the one
physical city with which I have felt myself in complete harmony. Somehow or other there was always a real kind of relationship established between myself and the smells of Paris,
the façades of a building, a person passing in the street, the
echo of a taxi-horn. Always, when walking in the labyrinth
of the small streets on the Montagne-Sainte-Geneviève, there
was a closeness between myself and those poets I love the
most, who are the most authentic voices of Paris: Villon, Nerval, Baudelaire, Verlaine, Apollinaire. I realized on my first
visit to Paris, and continued realizing more deeply on every
subsequent visit, that there only is one free to pursue one's
dream, to grow in harmony with one's dream.

It was in Paris I learned that the great value of art is con-
fession and avowal, and not virtuosity!

It will mean a great deal to me to have the water color
you destined for Jesse Clark. I hope it reaches you in good
state.

I haven't yet heard from Caresse Crosby. Thanks for giving
her my name.

Had dinner two nights ago with Jean-Paul Sartre. He came
up to my place and was greatly intrigued with your water
colors. He spoke with admiration of *Capricorn*. Did you know
that his play, *Huis Clos*, is being translated and scheduled for
a fall New York performance? I liked Sartre. Do you know
Le Mur or *La Nausée*? Sartre spoke a great deal and very
movingly about his friend Albert Camus. Did you meet him
in Paris?

Keep up the good work, Henry. I am anxious for your
next book to come out. Which will it be? It helps tie me down
to this continent to know that you are working on it too. My

love to Lepska. Is she writing or studying or cooking meals for you? Probably all three.

Michel

5/2/45

Dear Michel — I don't know Sartre, but now have a play of his. I wanted *La Nausée* for review purposes — and may still get it. I am also supposed to receive (for review) one of Camus' books.

I may be way off about Carco. But I feel close to him. And I love his vocabulary. It's highly evocative. Apparently not even the Villon passage moved you. Well, it happens that way some times. But it's important — and quite sufficient, I think — if only *some one* is moved. He moves me, I move some one else. We are all instruments merely. The work gets done — despite us.

Yes, I'm trying to do the whole *Season in Hell* — except the verse, which is beyond me. I may show it to you when I've done my last with it. Not to make you work — but to ask your opinion. At this moment, I am dubious of everything I've done. I can't whip up the courage to depart from the text. That's what eats me up. I lack "authority" — and that's a strange new feeling for me. There are some phrases I break my head over. I've seen another translation — it's no good either. Words like *Charité*, *Esprit*, etc. slay me. How to render them? Even *Rage*, *Ennui*, etc. Or *les Conseils des Seigneurs*. Or a line like this —

> *Des erreurs qu'on me souffle, magies, faux parfums, musique puérile.*
> Or — *je suis esclave de mon baptême.*
> Or — *C'est la vision des nombres.*

Enuf! If I can do this I can translate the Fourth Eclogue!

I am purifying myself to write my best on my friend Abe Rattner, the painter, whose work I admire above all living painters. Laughlin has accepted Vol. I of *The Nightmare* and the Colt Press have accepted the little study I did of [Jacob Wassermann's] *The Maurizius Case* — about 65 pages. I think, tho' it's a small thing, it will be very effective — as may one day *Murder the Murderer*. (I read this over from time to time — most unusual thing for me to do — and I always find it *épatant*.) I wonder people don't rise up from their graves and stop buggering one another!

I am now reading *The Book of the It* — by [Georg] Grod-deck — sent me by Durrell. He mentions frequently the ambi-valence of love-hate. This annoys me. It is true, I feel, only on a certain human level. Some have emancipated themselves from this ambivalence — and love positively — without a shadow. Why don't we fix our attention on the supreme effort? The man Groddeck is a psychoanalyst — like my friend E. Graham Howe — who also annoys me by talking of "the good" which war *also* accomplishes.

I hear again, and in full spirit, free, from Anaïs Nin. I am sure she will lose her fear of religion one day — soon. It's good you came to know her. But you have to be very subtle, very delicate with her. She has a fine nose. She resists every trap. She has to be snared open-eyed.

Lepska just left for a visit to the doctor in S. F. Everything's fine. She's a wonderful girl. I wonder sometimes if I deserve this bliss.

I hope you have received by now the Jesse Clark water color. I think you'll like it. It's different from any I ever did.

My warm greetings to Henri Peyre, as always. He grows on me — from a distance and in silence. A good tribute to his qualities.

Don't write me unless you absolutely have the time for it. I get all your messages.

It's so still here my ears hum. And a fog outside as thick as wool. And five wonderful kittens in the basket sucking away for dear life. The dog's gone to visit a neighbor. He's very much like me. I forgive him everything. He even *looks* like me!

Henry

1248 Yale Station
7 May 1945

Dear Henry,

All my heart-felt thanks for the two new water colors, which arrived last week, and which are now being framed. *Musique Ancienne*, the picture you destined to Jess Clark, is very different from your other work. I like it and shall hang it in the study. *Self-portrait* is a striking piece, which I haven't looked at enough yet, but which seemed more integrally you, more familiarly your style.

At present, I know the copies here of *The Little Book of The Perfect Life* are on reserve for a German course. Tell me which you prefer, English or German, and I shall send you the call number, so you can order it that way through the California library. The librarian at Yale didn't seem at all opposed to sending a copy to California through the correct channels.

For whom are you doing the Rimbaud translation? About a year ago, when the [Delmore] Schwartz translation went out of print, Laughlin asked me to "judge" the Watson translation and to recommend any other which I knew of. I had just heard then that Mrs. [Louise] Varèse (translator of Perse) had done a translation. It is quite good and I was under the impression that Laughlin was going to bring it out.

The *View* group have asked me to do a short study of Max Jacob for a kind of *hommage* publication they are thinking of doing. Jacob is one of my favorites, a real clown and angel, and I am undertaking the job with fervor. The *View* piece will

be short — but I shall do at the same time a longer essay. Did
you know Jacob? Do you know where I could see some of his
paintings?

Even if I didn't get much excited by Carco, don't think that
I wasn't moved by the Villon quotations. Every line of Villon
moves me . . .

The other day I really had my first talk with Miss [Frances]
Steloff at the Gotham [Book Mart]. How I liked her deep admiration for you! Your books are selling wonderfully, she says.
And people are always asking about you. She has many messages to write you as soon as she can find a little time.

I don't know exactly how to interpret your paragraph about
Lepska's visit to the doctor. Is she going to have a baby? Excuse me if I am blundering. But that news would give me great
joy.

All my real messages to you, dear Henry, I don't write, but
I know that you get them somehow. Last night I began reading
Death and the Lover. I shall write you when I finish it.

Michel

5/25/45

Dear Michel —

By *accident* (!) I had slipped an extra carbon into the
machine when typing these pages. Am now on p. 36 — and still
going. It is doing me in. I'm really exhausting myself with R.
But I've found the clue! (The "key of love," *quoi!*) I give
subsequently the words, from Baudelaire, which *precede* the
line I've quoted herein. They are very telling, his words.

I only read [Antoine de] Saint-Exupéry's *Pilote de Guerre*
the other day. Marvelous closing! He too *finally* saw the light.
On va où l'on pèse. That phrase runs thru my head continually.
But the line (out of *Saison en Enfer*) which plagues me so and

which I chew in my sleep, is: *Des erreurs qu'on me souffle: magies, faux parfums, musique puérile.*

Henry

I wonder if our good friend Henri Peyre will shake his head sadly when he learns I am now on Rimbaud! I see, gradually, that what I am doing these past few months, is to pay my debt (*hommage*) to the ones I adore. This is a detour, but good for the soul. I am cultivating my soul now with a vengeance. Rimbaud, incidentally, like Balzac, must have been a Neptunian. Read [Dane] Rudhyar's article in last *Circle*. Read it like a musician!

Did you know that Stefan Schimanski was very impressed with your ms. and has recommended it for publication to Drummond most warmly.

In haste,
Henry

My guts quiver like jelly — from intense concentration. I'm so deep in R.'s hell that I too am suffering.

Lepska shouts to tell you she just finished *Clowns and Angels* — *and loves it.* I reread here and there and quoted a short paragraph referring to R.'s *intactness* — leaving the white paper, silence, etc.

6/27/45

Dear Michel —

Not to disturb your vacation — just a word to say I won't send you the French books until I know definitely from *Town and Country* that they have no further requests to make of me. Then I will.

Am just finishing the Rimbaud — about 75 pages. I'm dizzy with it. I think I've done something! Can't wait until I get your verdict. (I owe everything to everybody — but yet I think I've made a contribution.)

Just received the first number of *Valeurs* from Alexandria — from [René] Etiemble. I like the reviews. I see he too has written of [Albert] Cossery, Sartre, Camus, et alia. It excites me. Camus, I understand from Durrell, has written something excellent — or is it about him — called "The Sense of the Absurd." I like Camus better after putting the book aside. He's a strange one.

In haste,
Henry

Big Sur
September 17th, 1945

Dear Michel —

Just a word to say that Lepska expects a baby next month and we will call it Valentin, whether a boy or girl. Strange thing is, the doctor thought it would arrive on Rimbaud's birthday. (I hardly know whether that would be good or bad.) Another thing — according to an astrologer who did Lepska's horoscope recently, not knowing her, not even knowing she was married, the baby is to be a prodigy! (An artist certainly.)

But all this only by way of telling you that we are naming you god-father! This entails no responsibility — only your blessings and your spiritual communications.

Everything, so far as publication goes, is going on roller skates. But I don't have time enough to write — that is, the work I want to write. But I'll get it all down before I croak, I hope.

I reread recently the 750 pages I left off at in 1942 when I came west — *The Rosy Crucifixion*. Am itching now to continue with it. Even I was bowled over by it. But what a reception it will get! I will have to find another place to hide my head. I hope you are well. I *know* you are busy.

Henry

Big Sur
10/1/45

Dear Michel —

No, I'm not going to hospital yet — I will one day, for a slight nose operation. It's Lepska who's going — in a few days — to Berkeley hospital. Expects baby about Oct. 20 — Rimbaud's birthday. I'm still on the Rimbaud. It's becoming a small book. And it's teaching me things — tremendous things! (For one, about my mother fixation.) I'm going full cycle, round the clock, with him. Have even touched on his probable life beyond point of death. It may be the last critical study I'll do. I'm fed up with "literature." Want to return to *Rosy Crucifixion* and wind up my biographical period. No easy task — like a prolonged weaning.

About the French books — lend to whomever you wish and then return them to me, won't you. The French are quite crazy about the *Colossus [of Maroussi]* — I think [Maurice] Girodias will be the publisher.

I've just finished the life of the great Milarepa, the Tibetan saint. Now looking over *The Perennial Philosophy* which [Aldous] Huxley sent me. Some wonderful citations in it. Like everything I read of St. Francis de Sales. Seems very close to me — like Meister Eckhardt. And how I hated that Catholic Church in his name in the neighborhood where I was raised! What lugubrious buildings our Catholic churches are! So different from Europe. There I loved *all* the churches. I love mosques even more!

Remind me one day to show you a letter from Eduardo Sanchez (A.N.'s cousin) about Rimbaud's horoscope. It will "silence" you! Overwhelming. (If only you could understand the language he uses. But he gives graphs too!) Now I have a horoscope of myself, as a gift, from Rudhyar. I am almost tempted to show it to you.

Did you ever read [Pierre] Loti's *Jérusalem* — used to be one of my favorites.

Henry

[card]
Big Sur
October 14th [1945]

Dear Michel —

Do you or Henri Peyre — or the Yale Library — possess by chance a little book called *Rimbaud le voyant* by Rolland de Renéville? Find mention of it in the *Correspondance inédite* (1870–75) of Rimbaud. Sounds very exciting. Now finished Part II of Rimbaud — may do a third.

Henry

1248 Yale Station
18 October 1945

Dear Henry,

I am mailing back to you the three French books — with many thanks for loaning them.

Yes, I have read the Renéville book on Rimbaud — and like it. It is a bold thesis, based upon books of magic and Oriental philosophy most of which Rimbaud never saw. Its main interest for me was in the "general" points he makes about poetry and mysticism. The application to Rimbaud is at times forced, I think, and even erroneous. Peyre likes the book less than I do. I do not own it, but I shall ask Peyre if he does. The library has it — and if that is the only copy I can get to, I shall make another effort to break a law and send it to you.

I have been thinking about Lepska these days and wondering if the baby will be born on Saturday.

Please send me, if you can conveniently, your horoscope and Rimbaud's. I am intrigued and overjoyed about how your book on Rimbaud is growing.

Today I received a copy from Anaïs Nin of *This Hunger*. Am deeply touched by the inscription and by her thought. I shall read it tonight and write to her.

I have just finished rereading *The Colossus*. It is one of your great books. I have marked my copy heavily and shall return to it again and again.

Have you taken up again *The Rosy Crucifixion*?

all my devotion, dear friend,
Michel

[from Berkeley, Calif.]
Oct. 26 [1945]

Dear Michel —

Baby hasn't arrived yet, so I am returning to Big Sur for a week or so. There I'll dig up the horoscopes for you. Yes, do get me the Renéville book, if not too much trouble. I feel it contains something vital for me. I keep holding open the R. thesis — the last word refuses to be said. Maybe I should have read more books on him. But I loathe doing research work. What impresses me now is the strong element of fate in his life. And I saw this again in Van Gogh's — the two run parallel — practically the same birth and death years! The one had faith, the other not. R. and Balzac have also great similarities — in their youth — the intuitional side, the excessive side, the excessive reading, the hunger for experience — followed by disillusionment. The older I get the more interested I become in biography. I see so many connections, verifications and corroborations.

Just read a cold, communist critique of Balzac by Grib (a Russian). If we use "life" instead of "capitalist society," we can agree. But no mention of *Séraphita, Lambert* or *Sur Catherine de Médicis.* A page on B.'s use of "mania." Quite good. Applicable to R. too.

I begin work on *Rosy Crucifixion* early next year. Impossible before. Am leading a helter-skelter life these last 2 months. Will go back to share cabin with Margaret Neiman and her infant. Lepska will bring another back. We have only one big room. We have visitors every few days — who stay over night. I go mad sometimes trying to concentrate. There is only one large room — about the size of yours — smaller perhaps. You can imagine what it's like. Now I have to search for another living place — we must get out end of year. I need a studio to myself, and will find one, even if I must build it with my own hands.

Met a most interesting man here the other night — Carlton Kendall. One of those talks which makes your head reel. Told me of Hitler's and Mussolini's interest in (and secret practice of) Yogi discipline. Is making a study of "genius" these last 20 years. Has been all over the world because of his researches.

Also met a German woman who knew Hermann Hesse. He's still alive — in Switzerland. I'm writing him. My best to Henri Peyre . . . To answer a question you put — no, I shan't baptize baby a Catholic. I want it to have no education of any kind — if possible. But fate will decide these matters.

Henry

Love from Lepska! She's fine but impatient. This beautiful city is "the home of the atomic bomb." And it looks the part. It is beautifully funereal, proper, clean, etc. The blinds are never drawn. Each house is alike.

[card]
Big Sur
11/14/45

Dear Michel —

I have just received 2 extra copies — (nos. 1 and 2) of *Valeurs* from N. Africa (Egypt). Do you have them? If not I'd be glad to send them to you or to Henri Peyre. I have moved down from the hill to the ocean, where I occupy a tiny shack, like a monk's cell — very much like that Van Gogh bedroom painting at Arles. When Lepska comes back we will occupy one of the convict shacks nearby. Baby hasn't arrived yet!!! It will be a Scorpio.

Henry

1248 Yale Station
19 Nov. 1945

Dear Henry,

Perhaps by now the baby has been born. I have been waiting for the news ever since the 20th of October!

Paul Weiss is here at Yale for a semester. Last week I met him through Henri Peyre, and I wanted to tell you how much I like him and how much his deep devotion to you pleases me. In fact, certain of his mannerisms and his voice remind me of you! He seems alive! I hope to see him often during this stay. Do you think I could ever get through his book *Reality*?

I have tried in vain to get permission to send you the library copy of Renéville's *Rimbaud*. If you know any librarian in California, have him try to get it for you. What you say about Claudel's preface is very exciting. I have always thought it one of the best essays on Rimbaud. That is the only specific writing Claudel did on Rimbaud, although he mentions him in almost all his books. My favorite book on Rimbaud, by the way, is by Jacques Rivière. Do you know it?

I haven't yet received the first proof from Laughlin — and the book is announced for Xmas. I suppose there will be a delay.

I have been reading all I can on [Georges] Rouault — and going through the journal of Léon Bloy (*L'Invendable*) where he talks of Rouault. I have often wondered if you know Léon Bloy. He was a Catholic in the real sense. The man who converted Jacques and Raïssa Maritain — and who spent his life in abject poverty. *Le Désespéré* and *La Femme Pauvre* are perhaps his best books. If you don't know them, may I send them to you?

I don't believe I have seen the first two numbers of *Valeurs*. Please send them if you have extra copies. I'll share them with Peyre.

Don't fail to send me a card when Valentin arrives. (There must have been miscalculation.)

Michel

11/30/45

Dear Michel —

Under separate cover mailed you the horoscopes which please return at your leisure. No, I never read the Rivière account of Rimbaud — do you have it to lend? As for Bloy — ah yes, I have wanted for 8 years now to read him. Send me the *Désespéré* first, yes — any time. I *know* I will like him. Anaïs and I often talked of his work. I often read reviews or critiques of him. And as for Rouault — he's one of the great for me — as a human being. He and Utrillo always make me weep when I read of them. Just had a letter from Durrell I must send you after I answer — it will give you a kick.

Yes, Valentin * is fine — was when I left Berkeley Monday

---
* Born on November 19, 1945.—*Ed.*

or Tuesday. So is Lepska. It was perhaps 3 to 4 weeks longer than usual in the womb and shows it. Very serene, features clear, no howling and wailing — not yet, at any rate.

> More soon,
> Henry

Mailing *Valeurs* too!

There's a Christian Science practitioner near us on the hill whom I respect and admire greatly — a Mrs. [Jean Page] Wharton. The nearest in female form to a Yogi I ever met. She talks (or rather radiates) REALITY. Weiss talks around it. I can't abide that book. Amazed you like him. If he resembles me then I resemble the marquis de Sade. Not that I dislike him. No, but I am surely poles apart — and I don't approve of that talky-talk talk talk and argument. *He makes me quiet.* (out of perversity.) No Jew ever possessed his soul in peace — not even Jesus, it seems.

> [letter from Lepska]
> Dec. 3, 1945

Dear Michel,

The angel-child has at last come to earth — having spent one extra month in the womb. The delay, I am certain, was not a miscalculation, but the willed desire of the child to remain just a little longer where it was happy.

Valentin — as we call her — is a good baby — and was born with almost no pain — and very little difficulty. For long before the birth I knew this in my heart — knew that whatever pain there was, would be sublimated in the wonder of the experience itself. During the brief period of labor, I tried to read *Séraphita* — and when I came to the lines in which Séraphita describes the nature of belief, I realized that I had a belief in relation to the child which I had never had concerning God —

except in my adolescence when I was in such ecstasy of love for Him that my parents had to use force to prevent me from becoming a nun. I write this to you in an incoherent way because the whole experience is still too much within me to be objectively intellectualized and verbalized. But I also write it to you who I feel will understand, because I want to possess the experience by sharing it. I wonder whether belief in God *can* be similar to true belief — faith about anything else. But it does not matter.

I wonder whether you remember these lines: "Belief — belief is a gift! To believe is to feel. To believe in God, you must feel God . . . The believer answers in a single cry, a single sign; faith puts a flaming sword in his hand which cuts and throws light on everything."

I have read your last note to Henry — and thank you for the concern you show about the late arrival of the child. And thank you for being god-father. She will need a spiritual father in this cold world. Henry writes that your Rimbaud will be soon published. We look forward with real excitement to reading it and discovering new illuminations re Rimbaud, who has become to me also an intoxicant. Henry and I — as you may have heard — began a translation of the *Saison*, and I am tempted — though a little frightened — to finish it alone.

I shall write you more about your god-child as soon as she develops more definite traits than a doting mother can perceive. I hope that you are well, completely recovered, from your illness and weariness.

> with much love,
> Lepska

a kiss for your forehead from Valentin.

Big Sur - 12/28/45

Dear Michel —

Enclose letter from [Lawrence Clark] Powell for you. Presume George Leite has written you by this time. Am looking forward eagerly to the Rivière book, for which I'm grateful and the Léon Bloy. Is that book (*Les Reliques*) of Isabelle Rimbaud worth looking into? I think I can get hold of a copy.

Am now frantically cabling Girodias in Paris to do what he can to save my little fortune from being completely liquidated by the coming devaluation of the franc. What irony if after all the struggle to get published, and now published royally (in Europe) I should lose all thru the devaluation! However, I am not really worried. If I lose in one direction I gain in another — always. More than any one alive I *know* I am protected. Blessings on you for the coming year!

Henry

———————————

Big Sur 1/27/46

My dear Michel,

The Bloy book came, thank you. Don't know when I'll get to read it, though. I did read the Rivière and found it most valuable. I will write more about it later. Am keeping it to reread and make notes, meanwhile trying to order a copy from Paris or N.Y. Is this, then, the best on Rimbaud? Not very much (I mean of value) has been written, I take it. I admire very much the way he analyzed R.'s writing. I would like to have done that myself. He makes me think. And excites me deeply. I almost wish to send you now what I wrote. I may have to revise my statements later, when I ponder over the Rivière more. Certainly I must go into his thesis, which is brilliant. Laughlin is bringing out Part I (about 60 pages) in the March anthology, and Leite will bring out a part of Part II (which is now finished) in the issue after the coming one. Tell me, hasn't Rivière's book been translated into English yet? Any why [*sic*] do you know? I should think Laughlin ought to do it, don't you? How true it is that R. is only beginning to make himself felt! And how he stands out among all the French writers of generations!

I wish you could get hold of Carlo Suarès' book called *Krishnamurti* pub. by Adyar in Paris, 1932. It would mean something to you, I believe. Though you probably won't accept K's ideas. Still, they will give you what R. gave Rivière, I think.

I don't know any one in all Arizona, unfortunately. In New Mexico, yes. Frieda Lawrence, who is here in Big Sur now, has a house — with guest cabin — at El Prado (near Taos) — about 8,000 feet altitude. I think she would accept you as a guest, if you wished it. They go back about April. I like Frieda enormously.

I have received five or six novels from Raymond Queneau, Paris, war time production, I think. He wants me to read them and see if they could be accepted in translation here. But I can't get round to them. I just haven't the time. So many books are flung at me — and mss. and what not! I wondered if you or Peyre, or anyone interested in French literature, would care to go through them and tell me whether they seem suitable for this purpose. It's a burden, I know, but on the other hand some people may want to read. Let me know.

Paul Weiss really bores the shit out of me. I wasn't offended by your comparison between us. I fear I do resemble him in many ways, that's why he irritates me so much. I can't stand "logical" minds — not that rat-trap variety, at any rate. And a lack of real humor. (Imagine, he finds those Guggenheim awards in the *Nightmare* excellent!) He does seem to have a great regard for you, which I am pleased to hear about.

I enclose an incomplete (lacking only a page or two perhaps) transcript made by Lepska of [Henri] Fluchère's preface to the French edition of *Tropic of Cancer*. He thinks I may find some one in America to publish it in English. Though it has its faults, of style, still I can not imagine any English or American writer tackling my work in the same large way, can you? I am always refreshed by French criticism, even when unfavorable. Powell is working for you, I understand. Would you like to be at Mills College with [Darius] Milhaud? Fluchère wrote me to go see him — they are good friends apparently — but I haven't the time.

Am delighted with my new studio over the sea. Often think of you looking out the window at the cliffs.

Henry

1/31/46

Dear Michel —

Just got copy of *Accent* with your piece on Gide which I read with the keenest enjoyment, wondering only how and where you got that "Neptunian" symbolism? You have a real flair for writing about others in an illuminating fashion. You make all other English critics seem dull and pedestrian. And whatever you say about "the artist" always rings profoundly true. You have achieved a sort of "critical calligraphy" now.

Also just received the May 1945 issue of *Horizon* (London). Wonder if you have read this most sensational book of [Jean] Genet's (*Notre-Dame-des-Fleurs*) which [Cyril] Connolly speaks of in his "Comment"? I've just written to Galignani to get me a copy of it. If you have back numbers of *Arbalète*, see No. 8 — in which a fragment appears.

I dislike seeing Giono mentioned as a collaborationist writer. His letters to me give quite another story. He maintains that Paris, the seat of the *littérateurs*, is controlled by the Communists who are against him.

Lepska has just gone to Berkeley for a few days with the baby. Am alone but busier than ever.

Henry

I *will* have something to relate about Christ after the resurrection in my next. But meanwhile — did you never read George Moore's *The Brook Kerith* and didn't [Oscar] Wilde write a cruel tale on this theme?

                                        Big Sur 2/10/46

Dear Michel —

I said I would write you about the life of Jesus *after* the resurrection — the period of forty days, was it, between the resurrection and the ascension. But the more I think about it the more I feel that it is important not to communicate what I think I have learned — a most tremendous truth — but to live my life in the light of it. I didn't come by this truth alone, I must tell you. Though for some time now I have been preparing myself to receive it, so to speak. By one of those strange coincidences I find corroboration, perhaps the kind few would see or accept, in Krishnamurti's words and actions. I found it again in the life of Milarepa, the Tibetan poet-saint. When you strike it several times in succession, and from such different sources, you are bound to take notice.

Unless I am greatly mistaken, no church recognizes this truth. That is another reason why I think it useless to go into it with you now. It isn't something to *discuss*.

I will now tell you a more striking thing perhaps. You may remember how in the *Colossus* I speak of the Armenian soothsayer I met in Athens, thru [George] Katsimbalis, and that I quote his most mystifying words about "never dying." I begin to see now what that meant. Or better — what it *could* mean.

What happens from here on remains to be seen. All I wish to stress now as before is that your friendship, your faith in me, means everything. I am almost frightened now by what I know. I guess you will understand.

It is late, I have just finished mending socks. I get up with the dawn these days. Am out on the road watching it come over the hills as I walk beside the sea. There is here a quality of the eternal which I have felt nowhere else except in Greece. It is most fortunate I chose this place to live in. Now it seems as though I shall be able soon to own a few acres of land and a house. From this anchorage I hope to sally forth into the world now and then by plane — I mean to Europe, Asia and Africa. But it does begin to seem as tho' I'd found "home" at last. Maybe I've just found myself.

Henry

1248 Yale Station
16 Feb. 1946

Dear Henry,

Your letter about the Rimbaud difficulty makes me feel better. Please don't say anything further to Laughlin. I am grateful to him for having taken the book, and still more grateful to you for having recommended my writings to him.

I keep thinking about what you say concerning the "truth" you have come upon. It sounds so awesome that perhaps I shouldn't even mention it. At first I didn't realize you referred to the life of Jesus between the resurrection and the ascension. Those were mysterious and wonderful days. Jesus on the road to Emmaus is one of the great pictures of the Bible.

In reading *The Happy Rock*, I was particularly struck by Richard Osborn's chapter on you. Is he still in Bridgeport? Should I look him up? I suppose you would have suggested our meeting if you had thought it wise.

Bless you for your friendship and your loyalty! Somehow, I feel very close to you in your new search.

Michel

3/6/46

Dear Michel —

Can you give me the name and address of the person who now possesses that last water color I made for Jesse Clark — I think it was called "musique ancienne"? I am thinking to reproduce it somewhere and would like to see if the owner could get a photo-negative of it for me. I'd write him or her myself, if you give address.

I continue to hear from Jesse's mother. A good woman, it seems. Certainly warm-hearted.

Just got some fairly good news from France. May be getting *some* of my money very soon. Also — this news: — 20,000 copies of French language *Capricorn* in the press now. 10,000 of my books were sold to the soldiers within 2 months after landing in France. 50,000 GI's asked for my books in Paris book stores. Only 6,000 copies of *all* the books (a/c Girodias) were sold prior to my leaving France. (I think more!) Anyway, interesting facts and figures. Now, after 7 years, I will touch a few hundred dollars in royalties.

As I said to G. [Girodias] — if I got the Nobel Prize, it would give me no thrill. One waits too long for everything to really enjoy it when it comes. Besides my focus is now elsewhere.

Hope all goes well. Expect a word from you soon — about *The Clown's Grail.*

Henry

March 10th [1946]

Dear Michel,

Just a word to say I am mailing you the Rivière book now, insured. The cover came off. If you would like to have it bound let me know; I have a friend who would do it for me for a song. I'll give you the address if you wish it. I'm hoping I will get a copy from Paris. Have read it over several times and made copious notes. It becomes more luminous each reading. The commentaries on the *Season* and on the *Illuminations* are astonishingly lucid and penetrating. It makes you dance inside. You use it in the classroom, you say. I wonder . . . wonder, that is, if the lads really get it? If they do, they are better than I give them credit for. Laughlin now says that if I remind him again, he will probably bring it out in translation in 1947. That's something, don't you think?

Love from Lepska and little Valentin. The latter is doing marvelously. Every one notes her awareness. She is way ahead of her age already. Three people have volunteered to do her horoscope — unknown to one another. All agree that she will be a rare person, an artist, most likely a writer. One says she will prove herself famous by devotion to a great Cause! She almost talks to me. I am quite crazy about her. Nothing gives me greater pleasure than to walk about the room with her and speak to her in her bird language.

Henry

[card]
Big Sur
4/10/46

Dear Michel —

Do you have the issue of *L'Arbalète* (revue) containing fragment of Genet's *Notre-Dame-des-Fleurs* — and could I borrow it for a short while? Failing that, can you give me Cocteau's address? Just got copy of Gallimard's *Printemps Noir*, translated, to my amazement, by Paul Rivert instead of my friend Henri Fluchère.* Did you know Giono translated *Moby Dick* and has done a short study also of Melville?

Henry

---

* Rivert was simply a pseudonym for Fluchère. — *W.F.*

Montréal
poste restante
7 April 1946

Dear Henry,

The French version of *The Grail* is in the hands of Parizeau, a new Montreal publisher. Would you give me Raymond Queneau's address in the States when you learn it? I have begun the reading of one of the novels you sent me.

I am glad to be in Montreal. It always seems like a foreign city, almost French. It is hard to get a room here — and I plan to visit a Benedictine Monastery for about ten days. While I am in Canada, my mail address will be "general delivery Montreal." These days one isn't allowed to stay for long in any one place.

Did I tell you that Paul Weiss has been appointed to Yale? I shall write you from St. Benoît du Lac!

Michel

Big Sur — 4/19/46

My dear Michel,

Just got your two letters from Montréal, Poste Restante. (How good that sounds — Poste Restante!) Haven't heard of Queneau's arrival yet.

Now about Leite and the *Grail*. I think it would be well to let George do it. Yes, he is a wonderful fellow — and a ball of dynamite too. How he accomplishes all he does is beyond me. Naturally, he has not the means and facilities of the big publishers, but I think his following is a good one. He is printing only good books. Began with the Egyptian's [Albert Cossery] book (*Men God Forgot*), followed by Durrell's *Black Book*, and will probably continue with Giono's study on Melville. It is possible he may do Rivière's study on Rimbaud in translation. His magazine is reaching out all over the world now. I think he will make good.

One thing is certain, you can rely on his word. He may not get things out on time — his only failing — but he will execute everything he promises to do and will always be a loyal friend. And he will make as good, if not better, terms with you as the commercial publisher.

I envy you going to the monastic retreat. Do tell me how you like it there at St. Benoît. Today is Good Friday. Good omen. Christ is risen! Hallelujah!

Enclose a clipping from Paris — please return when ready. This is the truth, by the way. Had it from my publisher. You know, they had to expunge five solid pages of the *Capricorn*, in French, and many random lines too, I believe. Could do nothing to stop it.

I just finished the Werfel book last night. It ends up with a victory for the Archbishop! Boring as it may be to you. I think you ought to glance at it some time.

Ever yours,
Henry

P.S. Is there one good *revue* there in Montreal?

Montréal
24 April 1946

Dear Henry,

Returned here yesterday, after spending 12 days in the Benedictine monastery, and find your card of the 19th.

No, I have never seen a copy of *L'Arbalète*, but I shall look around here for traces.

Neither do I know Cocteau's address. I suppose his main publisher Stock would know or Gallimard, for that matter.

Giono's short study of *Moby Dick* disappointed me when I read it a few years ago. It just seemed a straightforward *analyse* and not very critical.

Lucien Parizeau, whom I met yesterday, has taken *Le Graal du Clown* (French version) and will publish it in the fall. Parizeau seems a man of taste and enterprise. He is publishing especially poets and essayists. I am sending you his new catalogue. He will publish Sartre's *Baudelaire* in the fall.

I told him that *Circle* editions might bring out the English *Grail*. Do you think that wise?

The monastery I was at is in the congregation of Solesmes, and the plain-chant is done almost as well as at Solesmes. I had never had the chance before of watching all the Holy week services. They did everything! the washing of the feet, tenebrae, the blessing of a lamb on Saturday, etc. Many times I wished you were there with me.

I return to New Haven on Saturday.

Will copies of *Printemps Noir* be distributed here? (I should like to tell Parizeau about it.) I am anxious to see what Paul Rivert did with the translation. It must have been some job!

Are you well — and working?

                                        Michel

                                        1248 Yale Station
                                        29 April 1946

My dear Henry,

Thank you for sending me this letter and article of the Rev. Hill. Both intrigue me. I admire a good deal of the essay — except perhaps: "Man is God and God is man." That goes too far, even for an Anglican clergyman! I wonder just what he means. It seems to contradict his main thought that "man is tragic."

Am just back from Montreal and my desk is swamped with

work. This morning I sent you Parizeau's pamphlet. Tell me what you think of it.

I had a good chuckle over "une linotypiste dévote" and am returning the clipping. Thanks for your "Japanese" picture in the cabin.

You may receive the visit of Ben Belitt, a good friend of mine and a first-rate poet. He is going through San Francisco. I told him to say hello to you and visit with my god-daughter.

I shall write more when things are straightened out here.

Michel

6/30/46

Dear Michel —

I enclose a letter which came with the four books mentioned. I had sent them a list given me by Adriani — perhaps I sent you his letter? Anyway, what I wonder is this — would it be too big a job for you to glance thru their card catalogue (on Rimbaud) and tell me *what others* I ought (or must) read? I would not know by merely reading titles on the cards. I feel you would. I am making it my business now to read everything important on the subject before writing the additional pages. (You realize how few I did read thus far!)

The [Benjamin] Fondane book (*Rimbaud le voyou*) has left me dizzy. You no doubt have read it. A few more like that — with his vigor and acumen — and I will be radiant.

Suppose you are back at Yale again. Everything is fine here. My love from us both. The baby is about ready to talk and walk now. She's more wonderful each day.

Henry

[letter from Lepska]
July 1946

Dear Michel,

Enclosed is the list of Rimbaud books Henry thought he had sent you. The Yale Library has very generously lent him all volumes unavailable in California.

How are you? Are you working well — are you in good health — good spirits? Does your school duty take most of your time — are you giving any new exciting courses? How I should love to be a student in your classroom!

Your god-child flourishes like a lovely flower. She is an exquisite baby — extremely intelligent and conscious. She is sweet in nature — always receptive, prepared to welcome the world and embrace it in her smile and her little arms. She has just completed her seventh month — says mama, dada, baba, nie-nie ("no" in Polish), and sings delightfully like a thrush. She can stand by herself, crawl, and is articulate enough to make her needs known always. I do so wish you could see her before she passes this wonderful stage of being-in-embryo. Perhaps I shall come East with her in the fall. We are all well — all working hard — Henry on the *Nightmare II,* and I, occupied with house, baby, proofs, and now, Henry's mail. Life is good and full, and we feel will be even better, when we move to our own home — a mile away from the road, straight up a hill overlooking the ocean and the canyons. We think of you often and wish you joy always. A kiss from Valentin and Lepska.

Yaddo
Saratoga Springs, N. Y.
18 August 1946

Dear Henry,

Thank you for sending me the *Coda.* I passed it on to several here at Yaddo. Charles Miller had the most specific comments to make and I asked him to write them out for you. Here is his letter. Everyone who read the article seemed appreciative of what you are trying to do. I get the impression that they are applauding you, but haven't much hope that such a project will materialize. Several are sorry that you attack the Guggenheim fellowships. (I have often wondered myself why you bear that foundation ill-feeling. They have done so much good both to scholars and creative artists.)

I have been able to work very well here at Yaddo, despite the atmosphere of Victorian idealism and setting à la *Citizen Kane*. I have never been able before to devote so much time each day to my own writing. But I miss contact with "the world." Each afternoon at four I drive to town in the beach wagon just to have another view on the world — to become again a man on the sidewalk and thus recover some of my worldly identity.

As yet, I have not been successful in securing any living accommodations in Chicago. I shall have to move out of New Haven in early September. After August 28, my address will be: Faculty Exchange, University of Chicago. A whole part of me is still very sad at leaving Yale. The other part, the ascetic part of me, I suppose, believes that I musn't become attached to any one spot. So far I have certainly followed my ascetic principle in my various moves from Cambridge, to Bennington, to New Haven, and now to Chicago; all interspersed with my voyages in France: Paris, Brittany, Anjou, the Pyrenees, Auvergne.

I keep wondering if you still work on *Rosy Crucifixion*. The sections of it I have read make me impatient for you to complete the work.

Did you have a good week in San Francisco? How are Lepska and Valentin?

Michel

Wednesday,
21 August 1946

Dear Michel,

Here is a letter to Henri Peyre which you might forward for me, please. I don't know his address any more. And thank you for the suggestion. I would certainly not ask you to undertake this thankless task. If needs be, I will take a week or ten days off and go to a big library myself.

I gave [Père] Bruckberger your name for copies of the Journal. You'll hear from him soon, undoubtedly.

Do you know that the interest in Sade is growing strong in France? Some important letters and scripts were found recently, I understand. A religious student sent me a paper recently which he wrote for a North African revue, about Sade — in high praise of him. Came here to see me the other day. I meet some unusual French youths now and then. Seems to me a new type is springing up — and not "Existentialists"!

More soon. Everyone tells me Bennington is a wonderful place — physically, at least.

Love from us all.
Henry

an article by Claudine Chonez called *H. M. du pansexualisme à l'angélisme* just appeared in the revue *Empédocle*.

---

from the new home
on Partington Ridge!
Big Sur — Jan. 28th, 47

Dear Michel —

Returning from S.F. Saturday I found your letter to Lepska — and realized at the same time how remiss I have been. We only just moved into the new home — it meant a great deal of work for both of us — but it was well worth it. I only wish you could see it, make use of it.

No, I did not mention anything about your being a Catholic — I think only a very brief reference to you, in the Preface. (The book will be called now *Remember to Remember* instead of *The Egg in Its Prison.*) Yvan Goll and *Town and Country* have taken 2 fragments of the chapter. (See February issue of *Town and Country.*)

Caresse Crosby was here for a brief visit. I spoke to her about you — at some length. She would like very much to have something from you for a coming issue — a critical essay — 2 to 4,000 words in length, if possible — for *Portfolio.* The next issue will be out soon — doubt if she can squeeze it in — and the one thereafter will be from and on Greece by Greek authors. (She is printing 2 foreign and 2 domestic numbers annually.) She pays only a flat $25 — but I guess you won't mind that. You may gain a publisher as well. (She will bring out soon a series of "Books from new Europe" — translations.) Do send her your Rimbaud and any other book, if you can. Her address is 1606 – 20th Street, N.W. Wash. D.C. Will be there till first week in March when she sails for Greece.

The silk screen book I am doing with [Israeli painter] Bezalel Schatz should be finished by April. It will probably cost $100 a copy. It is really unique, I think.

I've finished up all the odds and ends and now have a clear path ahead. At last I get down to *The Rosy Crucifixion* — and nothing but. It's been like clearing a path thru a thick forest.

I do hope you'll be able to come out here one day. Valentin is wonderful. She walks now and chatters in her own code language. I adore her more and more. We have wonderful little walks together in the woods and over the hills.

When I get Girodias' long promised "next" check I will be completely out of debt – *incroyable*!

Henry

2/22/47

My Dear Michel —

Was surprised you knew [Milton] Hindus. That law-suit in Paris — too long to go into now. Trial should open any day. Now there has been formed a "Comité de défense de H.M." — Some good men on it. Reminds me of [Jacob] Epstein's tribulations over his Tomb for Oscar Wilde at Père-Lachaise. But the men today (French) haven't as much guts, I fear. The war has dampened every one's ardor. Anyway, there will be fireworks.

This must be short — I am up to my neck in work.

> Ever yours,
> Henry

My book will be out in April or May.

Big Sur — June 8th, 47

My dear Michel —

Your book was a consolation to me. My morale has been and still is at a very low ebb. The struggles I am now going through seem worse than any I had to bear before. They strike at my most vulnerable places. I cleaned up all my other work — which was considerable — in order to resume work uninterruptedly on *The Rosy Crucifixion*, but each day something occurs to prevent me from tackling it. To cap it all I find now that I am owed a quite staggering sum — in francs — which I cannot get here in dollars. And I am terribly in debt.

To change the tune . . . the last thing I wrote was a story about a clown (about 30 pages) for [Fernand] Léger to illustrate. It is to be a most handsome book which Tériade will bring out in Paris. It will cost even more than our silk screen book — *Into the Night Life* — a fabulous sum. But it's the story which I want to tell you about. It is the first time in my life I wrote anything to order. It was difficult — very difficult — but I wanted to do it. So I wrote almost blindly, from line to line, as it were. And the outcome surprised me. After I finished it I thought of you, wondered how you would like it. Two things guided me — the thought of Rouault and his clowns, and Miró's painting in which there is a ladder, a dog, the moon. I am not at all sure how they will look upon it in Paris — I don't think they expected anything in this vein.

All this is prefatory to my thoughts on reading your book.* I began with Rouault, then Péguy, then Maritain. And the last one I particularly enjoyed. If you interpret Maritain correctly, then he is another, like yourself, whom I must accept unreservedly, tho' for some reason I always pass him up. I was indeed struck by your remarks on "the sacred mystery of sin" — p. 65. And even more, shall I say, by the quotation on p. 64 from Baudelaire, concerning the "immoderate love of form." I ought to have known this phrase long ago. What an answer for my adversaries!

But the strangest coincidence is the very end, the last 3 lines — p. 114 — on the clown. That is exactly the core of my story which, by the way, I call *The Smile at the Foot of the Ladder* — that will go well in French.

I must thank you for clearing me up on the meaning of Existentialism. It is the first comprehensible statement about it I have read. You have a genius, you know, for making things clear. (Which probably explains why you chose teaching as a career.)

(This is poor paper. It's raining and I can't get to my studio. I'm alone and the baby is asleep. So I can write you more at length this time.)

One of the men you seem to admire and often quote is T. S. Eliot. Every time I read a citation from him I am ap-

* *Jacob's Night.* — *W. F.*

palled by the triteness and banality of his utterances. St.-John
Perse too leaves me unmoved — have the feeling he is only
saying "it" more complicatedly. But don't let this bother you.

I handed the book to a friend to read — a pure Jew from
Palestine — Bezalel Schatz, with whom I did the silk screen
book, and whom I have a great respect and affection for. He
read the chapter on Rouault and thought it beautiful. But wondered, as did I, if Rouault meant all you imply. What we mean,
simply, is that your views, though true and acceptable, are
far from the painter's thought. We understand, though, that
you are saying for him what he could not express. (Incidentally, is there any book of Rouault's collected writings? I have
read several things by him — and was impressed by his ability to write.)

Good, too, to read of Léon Bloy again. I never finished *Le
Désespéré* — but mean to one day. I mentioned the book in
my long chapter *Remember to Remember* — you will like this
section, on French writers, I think.

I must also point out a striking thing on p. 74 — on belief
and indestructibility. I first ran across this idea in some Hindu's book — or perhaps a conversation with a Swami — when
he spoke of Alexander the Great's rencontre with a guru in
India — good story, too long to relate here.

There is one strange academic flaw you cling to in these
essays. May I point it out? Why do you need to say (roughly):
Now that I have explained points one and two I shall go on
to elucidate No. 3? Why? This gives me an uneasy feeling
each time — as if I were in the classroom or at a lecture. I've
noticed you do it several times — in other books too — that's
why I dare to mention it.

I just reread a book I had loved as a boy — 42 or 43 years
ago easily: *The Lion of the North* by [George Alfred] Henty.
I wanted to corroborate a remembrance I had of a certain passage on Wallenstein — it's about the Thirty Years' War. And
I found it — the same passage which thrilled me as a boy and

which sunk deep. It had to do with astrology. Probably my first glimpse into that realm — coupled with the word "destiny," which later was so strong when I read Spengler. But just think — practically the entire book had faded away — only these two pages remained. It gave me a great thrill. And too — I discovered I could read a boy's book even now with pleasure and relish.

Well, enough. I am about to reread [Paul Valéry's] *La Soirée avec Monsieur Teste*. What a non-sequitur!

I was moved indeed by your *dédicace*. You are a great friend — of all men, I feel.

Devotedly,
Henry

---

219 Freeman Street
Brookline, Massachusetts
29 June 1947

My dear Henry,

It was good to hear from you — after so long a silence — although I always feel closely in touch with you. I am disturbed about your financial troubles. Mr. Clark, whom I saw a few hours in Chicago on the 19th when he and Mrs. Clark were changing trains, will be able to advise you as competently as anyone. Does he offer much hope? I suppose you have considered the possibility of going to France and living there for a spell.

What you call the "academic flaw" in my writing is certainly there. You are right: it comes from too much teaching, too steady an effort to explain things. I shall guard against it. Thank you for pointing it out.

I have to give all my summer (I shall be again at Yaddo, Saratoga Springs) to writing out ten lectures I am giving in the fall in Chicago on Surrealism. Here are the subjects I am going to treat:

1. Origins
2. Lautréamont: the temperament
3. Rimbaud: the doctrine
4. Mallarmé: the myth
5. Apollinaire: the poet
6. Breton: the manifestoes
7. Cocteau: the theater
8. Eluard: the doctrine on love
9. Picasso: the art
10. Conclusions (*Finnegans Wake*)

I am plunged into all this now and exhilarated by it. Did you know that I was given a Guggenheim fellowship? Have decided to take it beginning next summer, when I hope to get to France for several months.

Are you in communication with George Leite? I have written him three times during the last four or five months and can't get an answer out of him. He had promised publication of *The Clown's Grail* by April — and I haven't even the galley-proof. I must say that when I do hear from him, he is most cordial and friendly. I just wonder if something has gone wrong. I have corrected the page proof of the British edition (Dennis Dobson) which is to come out this summer or early fall.

It is pleasant to be back east. However, I have grown to like Chicago more and more. Exile fortifies me. I have been able to see more clearly into my past and into my future than ever before. And I have learned better how to live within my "inner" landscape this year.

Are you by now back at work on *The Rosy Crucifixion*? I take it that *Remember to Remember* is in the hands of the printers. Has its publication date been set? Nothing saddens me more than to know that you are harassed and beleaguered, you who should be free.

Do you have an extra carbon of the new clown story? I

should love to read it, and promise to send it back immediately. Bless you.

Michel

Big Sur
July 5th [1947]

Dear Michel:

Was glad indeed to have your most informative letter. Here
is the script * I spoke of — return it at your leisure. I am
beginning to doubt now that Léger and Tériade will want it —
probably not at all what they expected. I wonder what *you*
will think of it.

Yes, Mr. Clark has been most helpful and I think something
will come of his intervention. Even if I get a part of what is
due me it will prove a godsend. I can't go over myself yet,
maybe not for a year or two. But Man Ray is over there now,
and if the worst comes to the worst, I shall let him buy paintings for me to bring back and sell here. That's legal and per-
missible.

I just wrote to George Leite to get in touch with you. I
think I know what's what there. He is always on the edge of
bankruptcy. Durrell's book hasn't come out either, and I remember reading proofs on it when the baby was being born.
He means well and I know he will get it through as soon as
possible — but everything is in confusion there. His ideas are
too grandiose for the town of Berkeley, that's all.

Your program of lectures sounds marvelous. I am always
amazed at the wide range of subjects you are able to cover,
and with such clarity and conciseness. It is a great gift.

I always rail against the Guggenheim awards — but this is
one time they have shown good judgment. Bravo! I wish you
could simply do nothing at all during that year.

* *The Smile at the Foot of the Ladder.* — *W*.F.

Remember to Remember may be out in August — only returned the final proofs yesterday. As for *The Rosy Crucifixion*, I think each day I shall tackle it, but then some avalanche of pressing things upsets me. I never was worse off, in every respect, than I am today. I almost despair.

Lepska is going East to visit her parents, with the baby, just as soon as I can raise the fare. Maybe you will see her there — and little Valentin whom I adore. This is the one bright ray in my life, the child. I love her more than I have ever loved any one in my whole life. She's like a wonder child.

Just got rid of *six* people who thought it charming to visit me over the week end. So it goes. I really need to find a retreat — an inaccessible one.

Henry

Am expecting M. Cain, directeur of the Bibliothèque Nationale any moment. He saw the exhibit of our silk screen book at the Museum at S.F. and was deeply impressed.

[card]
Big Sur
July 12th, 47

Dear Michel —

If you haven't already returned it to me, please send the clown story (of mine) to Lawrence Durrell — 52 St. Alban's Avenue – Bournemouth – England — first class. Just had letter from Léger begging me to write something else. Which is exactly what I feared would happen. The Clarks were here — had a most enjoyable meeting.

More anon
Henry

(Tell Hindus, please, I can't write about his work now — too harassed.)

Brookline, Massachusetts
18 July 1947

Dear Henry,

I had been away in New Haven for a few days and when I returned I found the typescript of your clown story and also the card requesting it to be sent to Lawrence Durrell. I have just sent it off to him — first class. And therefore I have not read it as many times as I wanted. You must have known how deeply I would react to such a story. It reached me at just the right moment when I am submerged in a study of surrealism. I would like to refer to this story if I may, because it illustrates so many of the points I am trying to make. How I long to have a copy of it! If you ever have any more made, please send me a carbon. I am sure the French publication will be beyond my resources. I take it that Fernand Léger is to do the illustrations on your text. Did he make the suggestion about the clown theme? It would help me a great deal to know all the genesis of the work.

What you say about yourself, your state — financial and otherwise — is very disturbing. Has Mr. Clark been able to offer any suggestions about the money in France? The Man Ray project of selling pictures sounds very feasible to me.

Are Lepska and Valentin coming east? I would love to see them. All of August I shall be at Yaddo (Saratoga Springs) and in New York City for a week in September (7–13) where I am speaking at a conference held at Columbia. If she comes, I hope we can meet somewhere.

My prayers that the bad period will soon be over for you, and that, with the resumption of *The Rosy Crucifixion*, all will be light and happiness.

with constant love and devotion
Michel

July 24th 1947

Dear Michel: I forgot that I did have an extra copy, and here
it is. Yes, I did think you would be keenly interested in this,
just because of the subject matter. Yes, it was Léger who dic-
tated the subject matter — clowns and circus folk — because
he had already made his *maquettes*. Now then, the sad thing is
this, that just the other day he wrote me that he didn't think
my story would suit his compositions — "too subtle and psychological a treatment," is the way I believe he put it. Begged
me to consider doing something else, something in the vein of
les tropiques (which is what I thought he would say!). So, he
is sending me a dozen or more of the finished compositions to
give me fresh inspiration. I wrote him I would do my best but
couldn't promise and begged him on the other hand to recon-
sider my story on the ground that, aesthetically, the proper
thing to do is simply to match spirit for spirit — i.e. he has his
style and I have mine. But I am afraid he won't see my point
of view. I am also afraid that I shall not be in the mood to do
it in a different vein. So perhaps it will end in a fiasco. (Meanwhile my friend Schatz has an idea for bringing it out as a
little book — in some artistic format. We'll see.) Léger did
say I had the privilege of publishing it in English how or where
I pleased, after it came out in the French.

It took me weeks and weeks to write it — that is, to get down
to writing it. As you probably know, I have never written anything to order. But I did want to do a book with Léger — he
has been asking me to collaborate for several years. And
finally, almost despairing of my powers, I sat down one day
and began to write blindly, not knowing what would happen
from line to line. It took me several days to write it; then I
rewrote it several times, more particularly the last five or six
pages. As I may have told, I had to start with just two thoughts
— Rouault's clowns (and all they signify to me — and to you,

too, I now know) and that ladder in one of Miró's paintings — you probably know the one I mean. That was all. And as I worked along the title came to me, in French — *Le Sourire au bout de l'Echelle*. I wish I could have written it in French, that would have pleased me better. I knew it would be very simple, and as it unrolled in English, I was almost scared by its utter simplicity — as though I had suffered a relapse of some sort. You did not say whether you liked it — as a piece of writing. I don't know yet whether it's good or bad, as writing. I know I liked the theme and the way I treated it.

Oh yes, I should add another thing, about the genesis of it . . . Baffled as to what to write or how, I finally said to myself — "you have always been a clown yourself, you love the circus, you know it inside out . . . just sit down and write whatever is in your mind and heart." Perhaps there is some identification with cher Auguste. You know perhaps that when I was graduating from High School and they asked each of us what we intended to do in life, I said – "to be a clown in a circus." I had been the prize pupil throughout, beloved by teachers and comrades alike, but I also had been the bad boy — and above all, the clown. I used to keep the class in stitches with my antics and drolleries, especially when the teacher's back was turned. I made fun of everything. And later, at the [Cirque] Médrano [in Paris] it was the clowns I often went to see — they enthralled me. But you were the first one to make me realize the deep significance of the clown's role. I was literally stupefied when I first read you. I never read anything about clowns until recently. Then I happened on the queer life of the great Grimaldi. Well, enough. Tell me a little more some time of what you see in it, will you?

In haste —
HENRY —
6 A.M.

Yaddo
Saratoga Springs, N.Y.
8 August 1947

Dear Henry,

The last word from Dennis Dobson in London is that *The Clown's Grail* will come out later in the year than they had anticipated. Of course I will send you one of my copies as soon as I get them, but if you wish, I shall ask him to forward to you three extra copies. I think I may have an extra English script which I shall look up when I get back to Chicago at the end of September, and shall save it for the German publisher you mention.

Many thanks for sending me the copy of your clown story. Before I write you about it, I want to study it some more in the light of work I am doing on Guillaume Apollinaire. I wish it were already published so that I could have my students in the surrealism course read it this fall. All that you wrote me about its genesis is very important. It will help me to substantiate some rather obscure surrealist theories.

I am comfortably installed at Yaddo, in my last summer's suite: a big den (wood-walled, fireplace, casement windows, desk, chaise-longue, virginal, Roman busts) and bedroom-bath. It is a little wing, quite apart from the rest of the mansion, where I can be alone if I wish, or have people come, if I prefer that. Twenty-five "guests" here this month. You may know some of them: Agnes Smedley (specialist on Chinese communism), Horace Cayton (eminent Negro sociologist from Chicago), Robert Lowell (Pulitzer prize poet of this year), Henri Cartier-Bresson (the best French photographer who is here with his Javanese dancer wife), etc. You can see what a strange weird group. We all meet at dinner, the only slightly formal occasion of the day. It is not unlike an ocean voyage. The whole regimen is half-prison and half-sanatarium. I have the impression that we are all recovering from a break-down and trying to keep the fact concealed from the others. Each one works away in his cell-apartment quite certain that the inmate of the next cell is a bit crazier and queerer than he is. The estate is magnificent: I have real and unexpected pleasure in recognizing it from last summer: vast lawns, pine groves, forests and ponds, rose gardens and fountains. A *Citizen Kane* atmosphere of grandeur and railroad opulence. The mansion, all in monstrously bad taste, I now begin to like because I am familiar with it. Its spaciousness gives me a wonderful sense of liberty (after my crowded Chicagoan year) and that has helped my writing which is limbering up.

all love to you always —
Michel

Big Sur — 10/9/47

Dear Michel —

Here is a copy of a Preface I just wrote for the clown story. Merle Armitage and Edwin Corle are bringing it out as a little book next April, possibly with a few clowns (w.c.'s) of mine to go with it. I may need to borrow the one I gave you — will let you know later.

Haven't heard from Léger recently. He is supposedly thinking it over. I mean, using this story and not a new one, as he first thought.

Armitage promises to produce a beautiful book — of 2,000 to begin with — at $5 or less per copy. We'll see.

Things are looking up a bit now. I do manage to work every day at least. I've done some wonderful water colors recently — how, I don't know.

ever yours,
Henry

29, rue Cassette
Paris VIe
21 October 1948

Dear Henry,

Very pleased to receive your card yesterday and to learn the good news of Tony's arrival. Congratulations to you and Lepska.* I am glad that Valentin, my girl, is growing more beautiful and wise.

This has been a good period of work for me. Despite the fact that everything is in a bad state in France, for which no one sees any possible solution. I have been deeply happy at living here again. The beauty of the place is unchanged, and so often one is struck by the remarkable patience and goodness of the French people. How they can continue to be patient and good at such times as this, is more than I can understand.

I am working both on the Mallarmé book and on a new novel. I have written to Armand Hoog and Raymond Queneau but have had no reply. I shall try to look up André Rousseaux, whose articles I always read with profit. It is difficult to find time for everything.

The other day I changed rooms in my hotel in an effort to get a lower rental (prices on everything are shooting up) and they gave me the room occupied by Jacques Prévert who had just had a serious accident on the Champs-Elysées. He fell off a balcony and broke three ribs as well as injuring his head. The *femme de chambre* tells me he works on his films on the 7th floor of this hotel. Before this summer, I didn't know anything about the rue Cassette, which is quiet and narrow, — a kind of provincial street not far from Saint-Germain. But now I have just learned that the one time when [Stéphane] Mallarmé saw Rimbaud was in the rue Cassette. In the hotel that preceded this one, both Balzac and Rilke used to stay. So I live with a

---

* Tony was born August 28, 1948. Valentin and Tony were the only children issuing from Miller's marriage to Janina M. Lepska. — *Ed.*

few ghosts. Hemingway keeps a room here, although he is in the south most of the time.

I have thought about you often since arriving here. Your books are in every bookstore and I never cease getting a thrill each time I see them. You remain for me through these years our best artist, and I await all your writings with the same expectancy and the same deep convictions that I have always had. What is the state of *The Rosy Crucifixion*? Is it near completion? Are you working on anything new that I don't know about? Do you plan to stay on at Big Sur?

Michel

29, rue Cassette
[Paris]
1 February 1949

Dear Henry,

An excellent meeting the other evening with André Rousseaux, who is everything you said he would be: intelligent, kind. He is devoted to you and to your work. When he was attacked for defending you, he offered to make a selection of pages from your work which could be used in the lycées. He and I agree in our unbounded admiration for *Black Spring*. (That is excellent news, by the way, of a de luxe Chagall edition of it.) Rousseaux hopes very much that you will get here this spring. Everything is available here (as far as the children would be concerned) if you have the price. Living is very high, even with American dollars.

I will do my best about copies of your books.

Thank you for writing that warm letter about me to the fellows who are publishing *Zero*. Their first issue is almost out. In it there is a part of my Mallarmé book.

love to all of you —
Michel

2/18/49

Dear Michel —

I wonder if you have seen Albert Cossery's latest book — *Les Fainéants dans la vallée fertile*? I'm quite mad about it.

Please send me one or two good literary weeklies — that you like — I'm sick of *Carrefour*.

And don't bother about those books of mine unless you feel absolutely easy about it.

Money here is so scarce I am now resorting to "barter" for foodstuffs and other necessities. American royalties less than $1500 a year! Laughlin says I owe *him* money (sic). What a life!

But more and more my vision is opening up. One day I will tell you, in person, at length what I have come to understand by "The Christ Resurrected." And the difference between belief and reality.

I do feel sorry that you must cut your stay in France short. Love to everyone — and to the streets and paving stones!

Henry

29, rue Cassette
Paris VIe
27 Feb. 1949

Dear Henry,

I am sending you a package of a few weeklies and magazines.

I am working away on a lecture on *La Jeunesse Américaine* which I have to give next week in Montpellier, in Carcassonne, in Argelès-Gazost and in Paris. After that trip is over I will just have a few days left before sailing on March 25th.

The other day, thanks to you, Madame Benjamin Fondane called on me here at the hotel. Enjoyed her visit very much.

She is trying to edit and publish her husband's writings. Such undertakings are difficult today. Last month four more mazagines closed down.

Am distressed to hear that your income has diminished. I have often wondered if you have been getting your French royalties. My own financial situation is so bad that I have accepted to give one course at Bennington College this spring. Am waiting for permission from The Guggenheim Foundation. I think it will come all right.

I shall be writing you soon from Vermont!

Hastily —
Michel

5728 Woodlawn
Chicago 37
6 October 1949

Dear Henry,

At last I have found a small apartment, at the above address. I move in tomorrow and feel that a new life is beginning.

Yes, I have received all your cards and envois. Was very glad to have a copy of *Sept Arts*.

Bob Finkelstein has sent me some excellent snapshots of you and the children. Val looks like a wonderful little girl. When will I ever see her?

I keep hoping every day that a copy of *R.C.* [*Rosy Crucifixion*] will turn up. Thanks for telling me about the chapter in *La Nef*. I'll try at least to get hold of that.

What do you know about the store on 57th street which calls itself "Henry Miller store." I just noticed it the other day. It was closed when I passed by.

According to these snapshots — my main documents — you seem in excellent form. Lithe and strong. What wouldn't I give for a visit with you. Everyone else seems to get out to Big Sur.

At times I wonder if you ever have any peace and solitude there. The Mallarmé is practically finished. I will soon be showing it to a publisher. For a year now I have been working on a novel on the theme of Tobias and the angel. But it is getting beyond me and I am going to give it up for a while and see if I can grow into it. Have been reading Van Gogh's wonderful letters to his brother Théo. You know them of course.

my love and devotion to all of you —
Michel

5728 Woodlawn
27 Nov. 1949

Dear Henry,

Many thanks for all these things you have sent. I am returning the Wells letter to Joyce (an amazing document) and the letter of the Dominican Bruckberger. This letter interested me greatly. I remember seeing a few copies of his *Cheval de Troie*. He sounds like quite a man.

I am just now getting down to my article on Van Gogh. I hope to have it done in a week or two, and then I will return the Artaud and the *coupures* from *Volonté* you sent. I haven't been able to locate any more of the quotations you asked about. I am sorry and a little ashamed to have to report this. *R.C.* What a work you have done there! More than ever I am convinced that you are at your greatest power now. This new work is almost mythical. Everything has a new and more intense light about it. As always, it will take me some time before I can think it through and "realize" it, so to speak. It was good of Fink to send it to me, and I have passed it on to Kathryn Meacham.

I have gotten a great deal out of the revised passage on Van Gogh. Do you want that copy back, by the way? I should think you might try *Art News* with it. I imagine they pay rather well. It always looks like a prosperous magazine.

Am rereading [André] Malraux' *Psychologie de l'art*. An important book, I think.

Have just returned from visiting the Clarks in Cincinnati. Mrs. Clark keeps photos of Val and Tony on her dresser.

And now, to get back to work on a course on Montaigne I'm giving.

à vous de tout coeur —
Michel

Chicago
11 June 1950

Dear Henry,

I should be delighted to translate the French passages in your [Blaise] Cendrars article, if at the last moment you need a translator. I hope you place it in a good magazine. The piece itself is a moving testimonial. It is also an excellent evaluation of Cendrars the man and writer. It makes me want to read him again. I am going to try to get a copy of *L'Homme Foudroyé*. That I haven't read and you speak highly of it. I only hope that Cendrars himself sees your essay.

I don't know of any good book on Gilles de Rais and I don't own any Restif de la Bretonne . . . I would like to know the story behind the suppression of the French *Nexus*. There must be a story.

Until I hear from you, I will hold the manuscript on Cendrars. Leaving here Wednesday. My address until August 1 will be: 219 Freeman Street, Brookline, Mass. After that: Bennington College, Bennington, Vermont.

Mixed feelings about leaving Chicago. Wish especially I had been able to get to the West coast, to California and to you.

Has Rabelais meant very much to you, Henry? (You mention the English translation in your Cendrars.) I am thinking of doing next a book on Rabelais and am beginning to make plans. Do you have any passage on him in your current work? My book on Mallarmé, by the way, has been taken by the Univ. of Chicago Press and by Dobson in London.

Is the family well? And you? I keep wondering if the practical matters of your life are working out well. I know that your spirit is still soaring and that helps all the rest of us.

Yours ever devotedly,

Michel

6/20/50

Dear Michel —

As I haven't heard from *Harper's Bazaar* yet I suggest you send the piece on Cendrars to — Madame Jean Voilier — 11, rue de l'Assomption, Paris (16). She will place it for me in a French *revue* ou *hebdomadaire*. Little hope here. I trust you saw no glaring errors! Sending you an extra copy of *L'Homme Foudroyé* which you can return any time. I keep it just for this purpose.

Rabelais is one of the dozen writers who have meant most to me. I make several references to him in my book — nothing extended however. In one place I mention him *and* Dostoievski — "the two poles" of the spirit. I also refer to Arthur Machen's *Hieroglyphics* — in which he has much (excellent!) to say on Rabelais, particularly on the question of his "obscenity" — *more than obscene* — the "lists of words" etc. in *Pantagruel*. Read it, if you don't know it. John Cowper Powys also has a book on Rabelais — fairly recent. For me he is probably the most "rounded" figure in all literature — human to the core — much more so than dear old Montaigne. Samuel Putnam also did a book on him — *Rabelais man of the Renaissance*.

I'm just reading Balzac's *Sur Catherine de Médicis* — a very strange work.

Père Bruckberger (*Le Cheval de Troie*) is now in a Dominican monastery in Minnesota. May come to see me, he says.

Practical matters — money is scarce but we never worry and always have just enough. My earnings now (last 2 years) from N.D. [New Directions] books (6) comes to about $650 per yr!! As a matter of fact, I haven't time for such worries, if I *could* worry. I live so completely in my work and in the family that nothing from outside disturbs me. I'm finding my way — along the path — at last. Not a saint, no! But free of a hell of a lot which once bothered me. If we ever meet I can tell you it all better face to face. Much has happened — for the good. Inward peace and joy, I mean.

Glad to hear of the Mallarmé book. Do let me know when *Le Graal du Clown* comes out in French.

As for the Paris business — I really don't know what's at the bottom of it. Don't care too much either. If necessary, I can hold up the balance of my work to be published posthumously. The publishers are not taking care of me — God is.

I just wrote what I think a wonderful bit (in the new book) on Jeffries' *The Story of My Heart*. Do you know it?

In short, *ça va de plus en plus!*

> Warm greetings from us all.
> Henry

The children are wonderful. Lepska too has matured considerably since you saw her.

P.S. Did you ever see O. V. Milosz' *La Clef de l'Apocalypse* — *introuvable.*

Bennington College
Bennington, Vermont
17 July 1950

Dear Henry,

A week ago I sent the piece on Cendrars to Madame Voilier, to the address you gave me. I have almost finished reading *L'Homme Foudroyé* and shall return it to you in a few days. Thank you for sending it. I wish I liked it more than I do. Most of it seems fairly useless to me. Thanks to you, I looked at Machen's little book on ecstasy and read the passage on Rabelais. Am glad to know that Rabelais counts so much for you. I still feel fairly determined to try something on him, a piece that would focus on Rabelais as writer and artist. This aspect seems to me the least well handled by critics.

The general tone of your last letter cheered me. It is wonderful the way you stay above the world and undefeated by it. Your life of the spirit deepens each year. That is undeniable.

I am writing you from Brookline, but I shall be at Bennington from the first of August on. They offered me a good job there and I want to try it out for at least a year to see how I like it. I don't like living in the country and Bennington seems to be the one exception. I may also teach Friday evenings at The New School and therefore go down to New York every weekend.

Am just back from a week at The University of Connecticut where I taught at a Writers' Conference, the first work of that kind I have ever done. The fullest and most laborious week I ever lived through.

Give my best regards to Lepska. I am glad things are going well with her and the children. I treasure the little snapshots I have of you and Val and Tony.

Have you had the Dominican's visit yet? Is *Le Cheval de Troie* still being published? I want to have the Bennington library subscribe to a few French periodicals. Most of the good ones have stopped.

I still hear regularly from Bob Finkelstein. He is a most faithful friend and correspondent.

Michel

July 27th 1950

Dear Michel,

Yes, I did get Ayesha and I'm returning it to your friend in a few days — with much thanks!

Just spent practically the whole day rearranging my books, papers, notes, etc. Terrible job. Am now at about page 450 of the book and thinking to call a halt before very long. That is, probably issue it in several volumes, this much being volume one — or at least 5–600 pages. The damned thing grows and I begin to see that soon I can do it on the side, going back to the main line — Book 3 of *R.C.*, the unfinished Rimbaud, etc.

This morning a thought occurred to me. I need help — manual help. Maybe at Bennington you will run across one or two devoted followers of mine (for want of a better term) who would like to aid me. Here's how . . . You see, I plan to give an Appendix to each book containing the titles and authors of every book I can recollect ever reading. I have up till now put these titles down at random in a note book, as they came to mind — no order. Gradually I shall transfer them to cards, by authors' names and file alphabetically. Now then, for some authors I can recall only a few of their titles, often only one, though I know I have read more. I'd like to be able to send these cards (of the dubious ones) to some one who has the use of a good library and ask him to fill in all the titles by that author. Then I can cross out the ones I have not read and eventually give these cards to the publisher — in alphabetical order. I don't think there would be more than a hundred such authors, if that many.

I had thought to write Henri Peyre similarly, only for French authors exclusively. But it may happen that up where you are some one can do the French authors too. If so, let me know. I am not in a hurry — doubt if I shall hand the book (vol. I) to the publisher (Laughlin) much before the end of this year. But I have done very little thus far about making out cards — because it fatigues me to think of doing this damned work.

I think I told you once why I want to give the titles. Because I think any one interested in an author will be glad to see for himself what that author fed on during his lifetime. So far as I know, it's never been done. I doubt if I shall recall more than 3 to 5,000 titles. The job of remembering is fascinating in itself — and very helpful for reasons of "associations."

Before finishing Vol. I. I intend to include something on Gilles de Rais (!), Restif de la Bretonne, Sade, Marie Corelli, on "language" and a few other items. There is no order to the book, no chapters even — just breaks for sections. My life winds in and out. The two chapters, on Cendrars and Giono, are unusual in that they are exclusively about these two, more like essays on them. There is a lot of "recall" and a lot of "associations" of all sorts. The hardest and worst section thus far is the one on "Obscenity and Pornography," which I shall either revise radically or throw out altogether. I find I know damned little about the subject, and have read very little in this field — if it is a "field."

Let me hear when you have time. Père Bruckberger due soon. Is circulating mimeo. copy of his *American Journal.* Just got one. Will ask him to send you a copy. Quite interesting.

> Meanwhile — blessings!
> Henry

> Bennington College
> 12 August 1950

Dear Henry,

I am amazed and delighted that your book on books is assuming such proportions.

The card work you want done on your authors would not be difficult. But here at Bennington the library would not be adequate. You should choose either Widener Library or Yale or as third best, The New York Public. Peyre could easily have one of his graduate students do the work for you. If there is any difficulty about that, I will try to do the work for you myself if I can get a few days off to spend in New York. To reveal such a complete list of your readings is going to rob some future scholar of a lot of hard work. He will have to resort to proving how inaccurate you were and your library assistant!

I would like to see Père Bruckberger's *American Journal* if he has an extra copy. Is he staying long in this country? I should like to meet him if he ever comes through this vicinity.

Now I am settling down to a country existence. Live in an orchard, but I may have to make a weekly trip to New York when the season begins.

As soon as I finish a commissioned paper on Gide, I hope to get back to Rabelais. What you said about him stimulated and confirmed me. He's not my kind of author, but he's a wonderful "subject." I'm sending you my little piece on Van Gogh (in *College Art Journal*) and a piece on Valéry.

Someone showed me your picture in *Flair* [magazine] and made me wish more than ever that I could see you in Big Sur and see your growing family. Some day perhaps . . . All blessings on you.

Michel

Bennington
2 September 1950

Dear Henry,

In a week or two, I will forward your letter to Henri Peyre, who is in France, but returning soon for the fall term. He will receive your letter as soon as he gets in to New Haven.

I wish I could track down more things of Sade. Once in France I came across a copy of *Justine*, but had just about an hour to read in it. I have read [Pierre] Klossowski's book [*Sade mon prochain*] — which left me wanting to know more.

If you ever get the copy of *Empédocle* with the study of your *angélisme*, please let me read it.

I have just received visits from two fellows about to become monks, one a Benedictine and the other a Dominican. And both deeply interested in your work. They came here because they read the French translation of my essay on you in *Arts et Lettres*!!

Business begins here next week. I shall soon be existing à *l'ombre des jeunes filles plus ou moins en fleur*!

love to all of you —
Michel

Bennington College
22 Feb. 1951

Dear Henry,

Many thanks for *Le Semeur*. I enjoyed Hornus on you, and would like to meet him some time. That the Catholics have understood you didn't surprise me, but that the Protestants do, does surprise me. Pierre Emmanuel's piece on poetry I have copied out — because I am editing an anthology of recent French poets and am including him.

Yesterday Carlo Suarès' book came. I have dipped into it and want to read it completely. What do you know of *that* Suarès?

I am working diligently on *Les Illuminations* and often think of you in connection with them.

Is it true that *Plexus* is out? I wish I could see it.

Here I live in solitude. Almost no one on the campus. It's been raining for a week and freezing every night.

All of France seems to find its way to your mountain and your doorstep. And even by means of *auto-stop*. One day I'll start out *on foot*.

Michel

3/2/51

Dear Michel —

Would you like to see what the other French lad (also a Protestant) wrote about me? I have a typescript of his article I can send you, if you wish. This latter fellow, Albert Maillet — prof. of English at Vienne (Isère) — came here too, last year. A very wonderful, pure soul — a new type of French youth, it seemed to me. And an enthusiast about Sade, Nietzsche, et alia.

I am trying to read — or get hold of! — Restif de la Bretonne's works. Read *Sara* the other day (from *Monsieur Nicolas*) and was deeply impressed, a blood brother, I felt!

Plexus will probably be published shortly (in French) by Corréa, Paris. Don't know about English version. *Sexus* now banned in France "in *any* language"!

Henry

I am sure *Plexus* will grip you. Though style is much the same, the contents are quite different. A number of passages on the Church, God, etc. (No sacrilege intended with the "et cetera.")

"Et patati et patata!"

3/7/51

Dear Michel —

Here's a typescript of Maillet's article, which appeared in the revue *U-49-51* (Tunisie), Jan.-Feb. 1951.

Believe I was wrong — he *must* be Catholic, this one.

In the dumps now. Terribly broke, all teeth being extracted, etc. But what wonderful letters from France recently! I could go to the gallows with these in my pocket. Of this more anon.

Henry

P.S. Just read [Joseph] Delteil's *Jésus II*. He sent me it — after silence of 12 years. Towards end of book I laughed so hard I couldn't stop. I wonder what you'd think of it. (Flammarion, pub. Paris)

If you can read *his* French I will pin a medal on you. Never saw the like of it — in any tongue.

P.P.S. It's *not* a funny book — *au contraire*. The end is magnificent — *for me*.

Bennington College
14 March 1951

Dear Henry,

Thanks for letting me read this essay on you by Maillet — a more important piece than the other French article in *Le Semeur*. The introduction pp. 1-9 is less good, I think, than the real analysis of the rest. I would like to look up these fellows when I get back to France.

Be sure and let me know when Corréa publishes *Plexus*. I will have my *libraire* send me a copy immediately.

I was amazed to hear of Delteil from you. Last year I met him in Montpellier. His wife (an American) came to a lecture I gave in Montpellier and then had me to lunch the next day. Delteil gave me several of his books to take away — and I must confess that I didn't like them too much. But I liked him as a character — a happy man, I thought!

I'm trying to finish my little study of *Les Illuminations* and have been thinking of you a great deal.

Am sorry to hear you're in the dumps. Aren't you receiving royalties yet from France?

After five years' storage, I have my furniture again and your pictures, five of them, on the wall. It's good to be living again with them. They remind me of your wonderful visit to New Haven. I was there the other day, saw Peyre who tells me one of his students is helping you out with bibliographical work.

Tell me about the letters from France.

Michel

Big Sur — 4/28/51

Dear Michel —

I spent yesterday in bed expressly to read your new book* — and it was a great treat for me. Gave me a new insight into you. Envied your *planned* life, your beautiful work-hours in Paris, your deep knowledge of French, etc. (Tho' I notice one striking sentence — about the French language — showing strange apprehension, but one I know only too well — viz. "do I really know French?") How wonderful, too, that first lecture — Claudel of all men! (One of *my* "first" was an Evangelist — deep deep impression: Benjamin Fay Mills.)

And the rue de Lappe — here I had to laugh. I knew it well. *Tous les endroits.*

I began to wonder, reading you, if I had not perchance encountered you somewhere in Paris some time or other. We both went first in 1928. Curious.

Beautiful portrait of Mme. Psichari, and of Jacques Maritain. What a beautiful visage he has! *All light!* Tell me, which is the best of [Ernest] Psichari's books? I must read him soon.

This sounds scattered, hectic. It is. To begin work I first

* *Pantomine. — W.F.*

have to clear away a mass of c/s, answer loads of questions, say no! a hundred times. Am worn down before I begin.

I've practically finished listing *all* the books I've read (in 50 years). By authors, the cards fill a shoe box and a half — not so many, you see.

I'm searching for a book by *Léon* Daudet on the streets of Paris. Could it be *Le Pavé?* Do you know it, or have it?

Also, just read *Sara* from *Monsieur Nicolas.* Much impressed. Reminds me of myself and of Strindberg, one of my great early favorites.

I see that Genet's 2 principal works are now openly published by Gallimard. And no action by police yet. How do you account for it?

In closing I must say all over again how honored I feel to close your book. For the first time I "recognize" myself in a portrait by another.

Is your book being translated? And *Le Graal du Clown* — is that out yet? Don't forget me.

Wish I could say as did Maritain — *priez pour moi!* That hit me just as hard as it did you. Funny, I came back from Greece on same boat with him — saw him daily but never dared approach him. Ditto for Gide in restaurant opposite Les Beaux Arts. (Ghost of Oscar Wilde around the corner.) But your room where once Baudelaire and Jeanne Duval had lived! Ah ah!

Good cheer
Henry

P.S. *Et aujourd'hui — les jeunes filles en fleur à Bennington — ça vous gêne encore?* It's like living in a keg of black powder.

Bennington — 8 May 1951

Dear Henry,

Thanks for all these interesting letters. Delteil's I liked particularly. I think you are misreading his letter: it is *par suite de la ligne de ma vie*. (*Signe* is masculine, anyway). I still remember my wonderful luncheon at his home.

Louise Bogan's titles are:

1. *Dark Summer*, 1929
2. *The Sleeping Fury*, 1937   all chez Scribner
3. *Poems and new Poems*, 1941

I am asking Regnery to send you a copy of the Montgomery Belgion book.

I must try to look up de Fontbrune's work on Nostradamus. This correspondence urges me to it.

Do you ever hear from Madame Fondane? I liked her.

The Gallimard publications of Genet are *Journal du voleur* and *Haute Surveillance* which have nothing shocking in them. The other books are not allowed. I have often wondered if you have read Genet and what you think of him.

Le Graal du Clown not yet out! No, *Pantomime* has no translator.

Am deluged with work (*débordé*): 20 hours a week teaching, 75 term papers to read, housecleaning, meals, — and my own work! —

I miss you, always.

Michel

State College, Pa.
11 July 1951

Dear Henry,

Look in at Roger Cornaille, bookseller at his librairie du Minotaure, 2 rue des Beaux-Arts. He is a friend of mine and a great admirer of yours and a great seller of your books. He would be *ravi de vous voir*. Tell him I sent you. If you settle down please send me your address. I hope to get back to Paris for January and February. Am teaching six weeks at Penn State, and then return to Bennington. Am delighted you are getting back to Paris and that Valentin will see it. How wonderful if I could meet her in Paris! Leave her over for me. Bon voyage et mille affections.

Michel

Big Sur
9/1/54

Dear Michel —

Last night I was dipping into your Rimbaud's *Illuminations*. It's been on my shelf, to read, a long time. Never had such a busy year — and with less work done than ever. But a good year!

However — again, and for the nth time! I was moved to tears by your words. You have penetrated Rimbaud so deeply, and with such delicacy and reverence. Nothing gives me more courage or inspiration than to read you on *le poète de sept ans*. And what effort, what thought, what research, what weighing and balancing, has gone into all this! I am one of the few, I believe, who truly know and appreciate this fact.

And you had to be published by an obscure publisher! What a reward!

I don't know where this will find you — in some hall of learning, doubtlessly. Keep up the good. work! You tell us more about the good life than all the sermonizers.

I read more French than ever. Maybe we will go abroad again soon. I am happy in either place, fortunately. But I don't find "men" here — kindred spirits.

Did I tell you of my meeting with Dr. Paul-Louis Couchoud

in Vienne? What marvelous *rencontres* I had last year! Here I meet only pygmies, ant-eaters, sloths and slugs.

Well, blessings on you, my dear Michel. The children join their mother soon — for the school year. They are so wonderful. If only *she* gets to realize what a privilege it is to live with angels. Not that they are well-behaved! But what shines through them!

Henry

---

444 Ocampo Drive
Pacific Palisades
May 17th 1963

Dear Michel —

Bob [Finkelstein] just showed me your letter to him. I can't imagine what the trouble is — between us. It's true, I haven't written you in ages, but not because of indifference. Such things just happen. You are always vividly in my memory. And only recently we have been talking about you here. (I am here, at the above, a new home, with Lepska and the children.) Val is graduating from High School next month. She had selected three colleges she wanted to enroll in and Boulder was one. (But I think she missed out. But I'm not sure.) I was thinking how strange and wonderful if she should be one of your pupils. She has been taking French all thru High School — and is probably "average." One day she came home with Rimbaud's poem *Roman* to translate and memorize. I was in seventh heaven! She reads quite a bit in French. — of recent authors. Better reading given here in French than in English. She likes the French class too. (Tony began 6 mos. ago — in French. I coach him. He's happy over it too.)

Well, so much has happened since we last met it's hopeless to fill in the gap. I was supposed to leave for Paris end of this month, but now it looks like August. Going to assist in

production of film of *Cancer* there. At the moment, things are
a little complicated. But Joe Levine of Embassy Pictures forked
out the dough — and it will be done, eventually.

I haven't done any writing in *Nexus II* — only 100 pages
or so — *but*, I have been painting assiduously. I've now made
90 water colors in the last three months. I think I'm making
great progress — in my own peculiar way.

Bob has done amazing things with his bizarre method —
really astonishing. But — he doesn't really want to become
an artist. He's afraid.

I don't suppose you're likely to get to these parts soon, but
if you should, do come and see us. We have a wonderful place
— and I can work in peace here.

I'm not re-marrying.* But L. and I get along now — perhaps because we're not tied up. The children are maturing
fast. Tony is an unusual specimen — and handsome as can
be. An "athlete" — probably a future space man (sic). All
the best now, my dear friend.

Henry

P.S. Amazing what French books the kids are asked and permitted to read. Gide, for example — *L'Immoraliste* — and
others — Camus, St.-Exupéry, Sartre, I think.

---

444 Ocampo Drive
Pacific Palisades, Ca.
5/26/63

Dear Michel —

Can you give me exact quote *in French* of Rimbaud's "Everything we are taught is false" and from which book of his?
Want to use it on my new letterheads (and tombstone later).

---

*Miller had separated from Janina M. Lepska in 1951, and they were
divorced the following year. — *Ed.*

Don't have any of his books here — all in Big Sur . . . Have you ever read *La Chouette Aveugle* by Hedayat (Persian writer)? Pub. by José Corti — Paris. I'm crazy about it.

Henry

1320 24th St., Apt. 1
Boulder, Colorado
31 May 1963

Dear Henry,

Just before your good letter came, I spent an evening with a graduate student here who is writing his master's thesis on "satire" in your work. Frank Cebulski, a fine fellow, intelligent and well-read, and keen about his thesis. It was, I think, the best evening I have spent here in Boulder, where I have been living since last August. And largely because of you. So, you were very much in my thoughts when your letter came. Bob has been keeping me informed about you and this has always made me feel in correspondence with you. But I am glad to have the direct news about Val (do let me know what university she settles for), and Tony, and about Lepska. Please give Lepska my warmest regards. I always think of her on that day you left New Haven. I was teaching when you were taking the train. On my desk, when I got back, was a long letter from you in French, announcing that Lepska would come. And she did, just when I finished reading the letter. I was feeling blue, downcast about your leaving, and she seemed happy. This puzzled me, and I asked about her feelings. She said then, "Henry always comes back!" It is fine you are all living together again.

Yesterday your card came about the Rimbaud quotation. "Everything we are taught is false." I have read through rapidly the two *lettres du voyant* where I thought it would be, *Une Saison en enfer* and *Les Illuminations*. I can't find it, but there are countless passages which echo that thought. For example, in *L'Eclair* of *Une Saison*, such a sentence as: *Je reconnais là ma sale éducation d'enfant.* I don't recognize your specific phrase, but that means nothing, it may well be in one of these works and I will go over them more carefully when I get through correcting final exams. But on this quick reading, with your phrase in mind, I was amazed to find how many sentences are practically saying it. A major theme, and I hadn't realized it. My hunch is that the phrase, as you give it, is a paraphrase of passages.

Am glad you are painting. The three water colors of yours which hang on my walls are much admired. In fact, each time a newcomer appears, he asks first to see the H.M. paintings! I now have a [Francis] Picabia and a Max Jacob to accompany you, and a huge drawing which Cocteau gave me for doing a translation of some of his work. (My collection is really: art by great writers.)

I'll write soon again when I track down the Rimbaud sentence or sentences resembling it.

Michel

2007 House Avenue,
Apt. 19
Durham North Carolina
27 September 1964

Dear Henry,

This is a plunge into the past! In the forties, when we were corresponding a good deal, you wrote a preface for a book of mine you liked, *The Clown's Grail* — to be used in the French edition. I remember translating the book and I remember my excitement over your preface, and I remember having the preface translated. Then, the book never came out in French . . . Now, Indiana University Press is reissuing the

English edition in their paper back series (Midland Books).
I have looked everywhere for your preface because I was going to ask your permission to use it in this new edition. (The publishers are in 7th heaven about this possibility.) But I can't find it! Do you, by any chance, have a copy of it in your files, and if you do, would you let me use it? It would give the book a wonderful send-off, in this American edition. Originally it was brought out in London (Dennis Dobson).

I think the woman who translated your preface for me must have kept the original, and now she is dead.

I am now teaching at Duke University and have just moved here. My first contact with the south. Do you know anyone at Duke?

I haven't heard from Bob Fink in a long time, and wonder what has happened. This coming summer I will be teaching at UCLA and hope to see you.

As ever,
Michel

Pacific Palisades
Oct. 13th 1964

Dear Michel —

I was going to write you at length, catch up on events since your last, but find I haven't time for it. I am always snowed under — and today visitors to boot! It drives me crazy sometimes.

On the other hand, I really have nothing to complain of. God is good to me. Val and her husband live with me — keep house and so on. The boy Tony likewise. Lepska remarried some months ago — a professor of sociology in Pasadena.

I enclose something about one of "my" clowns. Will try another day to write more. All my best!

Henry

Pacific Palisades
10/22/64

Dear Michel —

Didn't know you had 3 paintings of mine. There is talk of getting out another album of reproductions. I'm just reading about [Jules] Pascin, painter, whose nudes are out of this world. Also reading about Élie Faure's life. I wrote a Preface in Hamburg (!) to his *History of Art* and now I can't find the original. Seems it appeared in *L'Express* (Paris) in French a week or two ago.

Also just about to read [Henri] Matarasso's book on Rimbaud. A friend of mine visited him (in Nice) recently and saw the entire great collection.

A Dutch friend (Henk Van Gelre) has written a book on [Nikolai] Berdyaev (one of my great favorites) *and* a 15 year old girl (a fan) in Helsinki tells me Berdyaev was a good friend of her father. *Quelles coincidences!* I help Tony with his French but find my grammar is off. Mixed up always when it comes to proper use of *de, des, le, du,* etc. Crazy, eh? My best!

Henry

Huntington Hartford
Foundation
2000 Rustic Canyon Road
Pacific Palisades,
California
Thursday, 5 August 1965

Dear Henry,

Although Pacific Palisades seems like quite an expanse of territory, I suppose you must be close by. I came here to spend the month of August and do some writing in this idyllic spot. Everything is conducive to rest and work. Once I recover from the strenuous six weeks of summer school at UCLA, I will be on my own schedule.

Bob Fink has given me good news of you, and the other evening with Franco Fido and his wife, I heard of your visit with them. This setting is quite different from Big Sur, where we met eight years ago.

This past year I have been revising my two books on Rimbaud (as well as preparing a translation of the complete works of Rimbaud) and now the two books are ready and will be published simultaneously in January by The University of Chicago Press. I am dedicating to you the study of Rimbaud, and I hope you won't mind this liberty. It is a small recognition of what you have meant to me through these years, when I first read you in 1940, and during those years when we corresponded frequently, and during the two weeks you visited me at Yale, and ever since then, when I have been keeping up with your publications, with the writings about you, and the eminent place you are occupying in this country and France. I still want to write a study about you: Henry Miller and France. That seems the most suitable aspect for me to undertake.

The body is sequestered here, but the spirit is still free, and I speak to you over the hills, and send you my greetings and my continuing affection.

Michel

Pacific Palisades
August 9th 1965

Dear Michel —

You are indeed fairly close to us. Bob has been talking about a get together — maybe next week (or would a Sunday late afternoon, dinner afterwards, be better?)

I am really flattered that you wish to dedicate the study of Rimbaud to me. You couldn't make me a greater gift! Am amazed too that you are translating the "complete works"! What a task! And how we need this! I once (several times, in fact) tried to do a very free translation of *A Season in Hell.* Had to give it up, beyond my powers.

Did you ever find out, incidentally, where that quote came from — "Everything we are taught is false"? (And how it was in the French?) I may use it on a new letter head, as below (a Zulu saying) — unless I use this Portuguese proverb: *Quando merda tiver valor, pobre nasce sem cu.**

There is so much to talk about I'll postpone saying more until we meet. I don't drive a car any more or else I'd come visit you. It must be blazing hot down in that canyon right now.

Am reading Françoise Gilot's book (*My Life with Picasso*) and enjoying it hugely.

Did you ever get round to reading Joseph Delteil's book on St. Francis? *It's a gem.* There's a writer also very difficult to translate.

Enuf! All the very best to you ever. You are like a spiritual god-father to me. Carry on!

Henry

"The time of the hyena is upon us."

[card]
12/19/65

Dear Michel —

Could that sentence from Rimbaud possibly be this (from a letter de Delahaye) . . . *Puisque tout ce qu'on enseigne est farce*"? (not *faux*) Louise Varèse hazarded this. She lost her husband [composer Edgard Varèse] just recently.

---

* Translation: "When shit has value, the poor will be born without asses." — *Ed.*

I wish it were *faux* and not *farce*. That's how I feel about what is taught.

I'm sorry you were so considerate of me when here. I did want to see you, believe it or not. Xmas is a hoax, a bad joke, but here's to it!

Henry

Pacific Palisades
Dec. 29th 1965

Dear Michel —

Can't quite believe yet that Rimbaud's "complete" works has been translated. A colossal task — should make you famous. May I ask you, please, to send a signed copy to my good friend — an ex-boxer but a great reader (who has read everything of yours) to —

Joe Gray
8611 West Knoll
Hollywood Calif.

Send bill for it *to me*. And let me know the publisher's name and address, so that I can order copies for other Rimbaud fans who can't read him in French.

The only one I know of living in Vence is Marc Chagall, but I never met him. [Jean] Dubuffet also lives there, I believe.

Val and her husband are vacationing in Mexico now. Tony still going to High School but, like his father, he loathes school. We live our own lives — pleasantly. Neither is a great fan of mine. Val read one book, Tony part of one — thus far. Doesn't bother me. They'll "discover" me after I'm dead a while.

I wonder if you know Maurice Nadeau, in Paris. He's a fine man — a true "intellectual" — and a great friend.

All the best now — keep in touch!

Henry

Pacific Palisades
May 25th 1966

Dear Michel —

Your two Rimbaud books arrived yesterday and I must
say they were beautifully presented. When I saw your dedication to me I jumped. I know you told me you would do
this, but I didn't quite believe it. What an honor! I almost
wept. Certainly these two volumes should be well received
by the critics. We have long had need of them. A pity the
one volume is so expensive, because the real lovers of Rimbaud usually don't have that kind of money. Whatever the
price, however, no one could ever requite you for the labor
of love that the book represents.

I hope while you're in France you will go to see Matarasso. His collection, I hear, is fabulous. (I met him in Nice
a few years ago.)

If you ever run into Chagall or Dubuffet do give them
warm greetings for me, will you.

Hope this letter finds you — have a feeling you are not
there now.

Meanwhile my very best and God bless you!

Henry

Pacific Palisades
11/30/72

Dear Michel —

I certainly have time to write *you*! Delighted to hear from
you. Of course you have my permission for release of letters
at UCLA. But are you sure they are there? I would like to
read them again before you publish them, if you don't mind.
(I don't want to hurt anyone by a careless remark.) Frankly,

I forget what I wrote. I write too many letters. Only now I take pleasure in writing love letters! Imagine, at my age.

I'm sure anything *you* write would please me. You always have, no matter what you write about. But have you a publisher in mind — a good one? These university publications are like duds, only a very few ever read them, it seems to me. *And*, more and more of those I had corresponded with are trying to do the same thing — publish them. Can the "market" stand it?

Have you seen any of my recent publications? For ex. (1) *Entretiens avec G. Belmont à Paris* (Stock) in French originally. (2) *My Life and Times*, pub. by *Playboy* and Simon and Schuster — handsome tome with loads of photos. Out in five languages now. Then two little texts — one *Reflections on Death of Mishima* (pub. originally in Japanese); the other, *On Turning Eighty*, a chapbook with 2 other small texts. Both published by Capra Press, Santa Barbara. If you don't have them, I will be happy to send you all of them — as a gift, of course.

Now I am making etchings and lithographs for a Japanese art collector. And a small film of my bathroom (the exciting photos in it; I talk about them — sort of diminutive *Voyage autour de ma chambre*). Who wrote this book? — I can never remember.

I must say, these last few years have been wonderful, in a way. I've reached a level of serenity, my mind is very clear and active, I have all my faculties, and when I retire (usually 2 to 3 A.M.) I enjoy a peace of mind which I suppose is the fruit of much struggle, frustration and despair. I read only about an hour a day (in bed only) — and what wonderful books — all kinds, all subjects, *very few novels*. Best of all, I am in love, madly in love, and it is shared.

Soon, by the way, Stock will bring out a book by an astrological friend of mine in Switzerland — an Astrological Portrait. Author — Mme. Jacqueline Langmann. Do you know her, or of her?

Excuse me for writing so much about myself, but I know you want news, and it seems years and years since we really corresponded.

Tony had no idea that Barney Rosset [publisher of Grove Press] thought that much of him. Both Tony and Val are fine. Val keeps up the old house in Big Sur. Tony is working as an attendant at a gas station. Sounds bad, but I know he'll grow into something unusual with time. He's more independent, more of a rebel than I was at his age. Reads good *and* bad literature — and knows the difference. I still urge people to read less and less, not more and more.

Not long ago I read a book about the Gnostics of old (by Jacques Lacarrière) and was deeply impressed. If I had lived then I think I would have been one. They said that this world of ours is "a cosmic mistake." I love that, for everything about our world, good or bad, seems utterly crazy to me, and upside down.

Well, enough for now. Let me hear from you soon again. Meanwhile all good wishes. I hope you are well and, if not happy, content with your lot.

Henry

Appendix

Henry Miller and French Writers
by Wallace Fowlie

Henry Miller has always been impatient to receive books he hears about, and impatient to distribute to his friends books he has read and liked. In all of his writings: books, articles, interviews, letters, — there is a medley of titles and delighted memories associated with books. The memories and titles overlap and intertwine. Forty-five years ago his discovery of France, of Paris and the Villa Seurat was also the discovery of himself and the discovery of French writers. Lawrence Durrell thought of him as "the American Villon" when he imagined Henry walking in the streets of Paris. It is an admirable analogy because of a similar sensitivity and a similar aggressiveness that helped to form the character of the fifteenth-century French poet and the twentieth-century American writer.

After the interval of several years, when Henry Miller read over his letters to me, letters which he had somewhat forgotten, he was struck by the many references he had made to French literature and to French writers. It occurs to me that it might not be out of place to comment here briefly on the role played by French writers in Miller's life, to indicate, even summarily, the particular form of attachment he has developed through the years to French literary figures. This would serve, then, as a coda to many of the letters in this collection and to other writings, both letters and books.

If my point of departure is the letters themselves addressed to me, I bear in mind a richer deeper source central to the character of my friend who learned early in life a way of opening himself to all influences. Everything nourishes this man, and perhaps particularly — he has said this on various occasions — what he does not understand or what he understands imperfectly. French, an acquired language, was not always clear to him. He grew to read it easily and well; but there was always, lurking in his mind, as in the minds of many of us, the thought that perhaps he does not understand French as well as he thinks, as well as others tell him he understands it. This very difficulty has been a goad, a challenge to work even harder on a language that attracted him strongly, and on a culture which he has appropriated for himself and used — monumentally — in his work.

The five or six French writers who return often in his letters and books do not represent one type of writer. I had thought this first: that Henry was attracted in particular to the lusty lover of life — to Rabelais, for example, to the man who pursues truth and develops in that pursuit a great power of language. Among the older writers Rabelais is the obvious key figure for Henry. He prefers the language of Rabelais to the language of Joyce; and among the moderns Jean Giono would come close to Rabelais, as a contemporary self-liberator who sings joyously of the world's beauty and man's power. Rabelais and Giono, separated by four centuries, would easily illustrate that category of writer, which is to some extent Henry Miller's also, of free spirit believing in the brotherhood of man and the oneness of everything. "There is no wall between Giono's spirit and my own," he writes in *Books in My Life.*

Giono appeared to Miller as a French Whitman. The long lyric novels *Le Chant du Monde* and *Que ma joie demeure,* in their particular form: part story, part prose poem, recall the novels of Miller himself. Writing is an act that gives happiness to both men. The intensity of their lives has made them attentive to what they would call the obscure forces in the world of nature and in the world of men. Both advocate a return to an ancient lost simplicity in living. The mythological past seems truer to them than our machine civilization.

Miller has often expressed his admiration for Blaise Cendrars, and his gratitude for Cendrars' review of *Tropic of Cancer*, the first to appear. *Moravagine* was one of the first books Henry began reading directly in French when he settled down in Paris in the late twenties. The two men often met in the thirties (it was Cendrars who looked up Henry Miller) and as time went on and Miller became well acquainted with both the man and his books, he began looking upon him as a "continent" in contemporary literature. As in the style of Rabelais and Giono, there is in Cendrars a robustness, a use of full colors, a sense of exploration, an apology for action and stylistic effects that are also in Miller. Cendrars and Miller are together in their apartness, in their isolation from the more "literary" writers of the forties and fifties. They are both cosmopolitans who condemn art for art's sake, who live first and then write about their life, who, because they are adventurers in life, enjoy in their writing an ample use of digressions. They were the pioneers, the real forerunners of what is called today in France *alittérature*.

In *Wisdom of the Heart*, Henry Miller pays particular tribute to Blaise Cendrars. Because of the honesty of his heart, Cendrars appeared to Miller as the most solitary of men, the exemplary voyager, the visionary, and . . . the most liberated. In that turbulent kind of writing we associate with both authors, Miller refers to Cendrars' "battered mug" and the blind tragic defiance of the Greeks he sees in his French friend.

Only partially could Balzac be ascribed to this first and perhaps leading category of French writer who is the vigorous lover of life and whose style comes from an abundance of words and facility in creative power. Miller seems attracted to Balzac for other reasons than for the opulence and the expansiveness of the *Comédie Humaine*. He finds in the two novels he has commented on the most frequently, *Séraphita* and *Louis Lambert*, evidences of worlds that are unseen and unknown. The special vision vouchsafed to Balzac made him for Miller a spiritual exile.

He finds that the occultism in *Séraphita*, for example, is not purely intellectual. It is rather a force, a knowledge coming from the heart. Balzac believed in the dawn of a new world. This conviction, more than any other, moved and excited Henry Miller who has expressed similar theories concerning the end of our particular civilization and the vision of a world to come. In Balzac's spiritual cosmogony, all will be one, although there will be catastrophes and sacrifices before such an advent. The character of Louis Lambert is seen by Miller to be Balzac's own self, his angelic self which was killed in his struggle with the world.

Every aspect of Balzac's biography has fascinated Miller. He often refers to the Collège de Vendôme where Balzac studied as a boy as that typical school where poets are murdered. This was the novelist's first initiation to the futility of western life with its emphasis on doing rather than being. When that dawn comes which Balzac refers to, it will alter the essence of man's nature. This means for Miller that the wisdom of the heart will rule in the ages to come. Balzac once revered saints and mystics, as Henry Miller does in our present age. The French novelist saw everything in the world — organic and inorganic — as being possessed with life.

The study of Balzac by Ernst-Robert Curtius served Miller both as inspiration in his appreciation of Balzac, and as a source of important information and documentation. In his study of French writers, he often isolates one critic who has been especially useful to him and pays him a debt of gratitude: Curtius for Balzac, John Cowper Powys for Rabelais, Enid Starkie for Rimbaud.

In the fall 1944 issue of *Accent*, Henry Miller contributed

an article on Lautréamont for which he used as a title a phrase
from canto IV, stanza 7, of *Les Chants de Maldoror*: "Let us
be content with three little new-born elephants." The passage
in question leads into a sentence on the two neighboring monarchs, Maldoror and God. Writing in the same style that characterizes his pages on Rimbaud and D. H. Lawrence, Miller adds
personal jibes and quips to his principal argument. He states
that the Anglo-Saxon temperament, with its love for violence
and pornography and cruelty, may one day make *Les Chants
de Maldoror* a best-seller. He refers to Judge Woolsey's decision
in favor of Joyce's *Ulysses* against the United States, which
made 1933 a banner year in the war waged on censorship, and
opened up the way to the publication of such works as those
of Lautréamont and Sade.

He names together Baudelaire, Rimbaud, and Lautréamont
as the three sinister-looking stars of the nineteenth century who
make it for us today one of the most illustrious literary centuries. Miller reminds us that there were other major writers:
Whitman, Blake, Dostoevsky, Kierkegaard, and Nietzsche; but
he believes the three "bandits," as he calls Baudelaire, Rimbaud, and Lautréamont, have been sanctified in a very special
way. They were angels in disguise.

Henry Miller points out the beginning of canto IV in *Maldoror* as being something unique in literature. "A man or a
stone or a tree is going to begin this canto." (*C'est un homme
ou une pierre ou un arbre qui va commencer le 4e chant.*)
Such a sentence, although written in French, goes beyond
French literature toward something that seems rather to appear
Aztec-like, Patagonian-like. Miller refers to the passage on
God's hair left in the bordello, and the lovemaking scene between the female shark and Maldoror. The moment in history
when Lautréamont lived was so sad that the genius had to rise
above it, like a bird in the air, like an albatross. The literary
genres, with their precise definitions and forms, have little
meaning when applied to Lautréamont. An analysis of the

themes and scaffoldings in *Les Chants* will do little good. What counts, says Miller, is the fact that a man is crucifying himself in the work. Tenderness and humility are also there. In speaking directly to his reader, Miller says that if you have never taken a trip to nadir, here is your chance.

The monstrousness of Lautréamont's dream is more real for Miller than the imbecilic acts of man's daily life. The absolute evil sung by Lautréamont and perpetrated by his character Maldoror is more pure than the devious counterfeit forms of evil that we encounter each day. The reading of Lautréamont is therapeutic for Henry Miller. It provides a clearing of the air, a means by which we may see in perspective the dual role throughout history of the two monarchs, of God and man.

In early 1932, when Henry left Paris for Dijon where he had accepted a teaching post at the lycée Carnot as *répétiteur d'anglais*, Anaïs Nin had given him a copy of Proust's *A la recherche du temps perdu*. She must have had premonitions of the possible dreariness and monotony of such a position for Henry, and provided him with a long work with which to fill some of the empty hours. In several of his letters to Miss Nin, he comments on his reading of Proust, on passages and themes that would seem to come especially from *La Prisonnière*. He speaks of reading "a big dose of Proust" at the Café Miroir. As he works his way through the dense text, he has the impression of "sundering veils" and seeing into "reality." He feels saturated with Albertine. The theme of jealousy, closely associated with the character of Albertine, is so richly orchestrated that he calls it a "symphonic treatment" of jealousy, "so immense, so thoroughly annotated and documented that it exhausts the subject." The preoccupations with Proust, and especially with the theme of jealousy, is carried over from letter to letter. Miller compares the power of the form that Proust found for his treatment of jealousy with the accomplishment of Bach in music. One of his final notations — and one of the strongest — corroborates what many readers of Proust, myself included, have felt: "the man robs me of my very own experiences, sensations, reactions."

Henry Miller has carefully explained that the origin of his study of Rimbaud (*The Time of the Assassins*) came from his dissatisfaction with an attempt to translate *Une saison en enfer.* I suspect that this was the earliest and the only attempt of Miller to translate. At least to translate a major text. But this detailed study of words brought him into the closest possible contact with a text that has stimulated and held him perhaps more firmly than any other single text. Every line of Rimbaud seems to awaken in him echoes and reminiscences of his own life and his own thoughts. As Baudelaire found in Poe, so Miller found in Rimbaud confirmation and emotions and illuminations.

He first heard of Rimbaud at the age to thirty-six in Brooklyn. Six or seven years later, at Louveciennes, at Anaïs Nin's house outside of Paris, he looked at the texts of Rimbaud, but not too attentively. It was a full creative moment for Miller, and he was reluctant to sacrifice time to any occupation save his own writing. At Beverly Glen, in California, where he settled down briefly in 1943, he began reading about Rimbaud, and was struck, in his first contact with the poet's biography, by the endless parallels between Rimbaud's life and his own. The parallels were there, but each had moved in an opposite direction: Rimbaud, from literature to life, and Miller from life to literature.

He began writing out phrases from Rimbaud on the walls of rooms where he lived. Thanks to the study of Rimbaud, the word "poet" took on a fuller meaning, as representing the man who dwells in the spirit and the imagination. He saw the poet Rimbaud also as the pariah, as the anomaly, as the symbol of the disruptive forces now making themselves felt in the world. In Rimbaud, Henry rediscovered his own plight in the world.

Some of the traits admired in Cendrars and Céline are more movingly, more deeply discovered in Rimbaud, and Miller acknowledges that the French poet heads the list of those rebels and failures he loves and identifies with. The very life of the rebel-failure is the proving ground of the spirit. In no other writer has Miller seen himself so clearly as in Rimbaud. Despite the fogs of a language he never totally mastered (no foreigner ever totally masters, we might say), he admits that Rimbaud articulated nothing that is alien to him.

The latter half of the nineteenth century is looked upon by Miller as an accursed period in history. With Rimbaud he associated Van Gogh and groups them as two imprisoned spirits. But the entire century for Miller is constellated with demonic figures in Europe: Nerval, Kierkegaard, Lautréamont, Nietzsche, Dostoevsky. And Rimbaud, more dramatically than all the others, is a light which annihilates when it does not exalt or illumine.

Frequently in writing of Rimbaud, Miller returns to the letters written to the poet's mother and sister when he was travelling at a great distance from Charleville, and seeking some form of employment. A genius, such as Rimbaud, looking for employment, is for Miller the saddest sight in the world. The voyages through various countries of Europe, in Ethiopia and Arabia, are called by Miller, Rimbaud's *tour du monde . . .* on an empty stomach. And he points out the "sheer dementia" that picture must represent to most Frenchmen cultivating their gardens. Every time he picks up Rimbaud's book, or every time he rereads the haunting passages he copied out on the wall, Miller is touched by the poet's purity. The future belongs to the poet, Miller believes, as once the future belonged to Christ's acceptance of the Cross, or to Joan of Arc's mission. Miller's claim is extreme when he writes that the Rimbaud type will replace the Hamlet and the Faust type.

Rimbaud as prophet and mystic for Miller is the poet who exalts the created universe where everything is a sign. Only the type of writer that Rimbaud was is endowed with sufficient vision to interpret the signs. Miller found in Rimbaud that paradox of paradoxes which both distressed and inflamed him: the poet cursed by his world, *le maudit*, because he was angelic, the type of innocent walking in the midst of the world's corruption. Of all the arts, poetry is the one in which the power of man's spirit is best measured. This is exactly the confirmation that Miller discovered on the pages of Rimbaud in the passages that seemed to him pure, autonomous, liberated from all traces of vulgarity and compromise.

Prophecy is the most ancient temptation of man. Henry Miller has always welcomed that temptation. Among all the prophets who preceded him was Rimbaud:

> *Elle est retrouvée. — Quoi?*
> *L'éternité ...*

Such words as these confirmed Miller's belief that there is no need to escape from life, that there is in fact no way to escape. Man remains in permanent contact with the world, and learns, if he is the writer, to express this contact in words that are jubilant and strong, in phrases that are fecund and active, in music that is universal and sonorous, where every daily act, no matter how trivial, will relive and resound in the strange words of the writer. For Rimbaud: it was meaning found in the inns and streets of Belgium, the fairy-like fantasies of childhood, the memories of clear summer dawns. For Henry Miller: it was meaning found in the Villa Seurat and the streets of Paris, the American Telegraph Company, the insecurity of dangerous freedom, and the reading in a foreign language of so many different spirits: Rabelais, Sade, Nerval, Élie Faure, Céline, Arthur Rimbaud.

April 1974

Wall Sentences
from H.M. to W.F.

This was pinned to the kitchen wall so that I could look at it when cooking. I send it to you as a little memento.

"The cleanest expression is that which finds no sphere worthy of itself and makes one."

WALT WHITMAN

"No one will get at my verses who insists upon viewing them as a literary performance, or attempt at such performance, or as aiming mainly toward art or aestheticism."

WALT WHITMAN

"Moi, moi, qui me suis dit mage ou ange, dispensé de toute morale, je suis rendu au sol."

RIMBAUD

"If I had no other book than only the book which I am myself so I have books enough."

JACOB BOEHME

"I enjoy a certain consideration because of my humane behavior. I have never injured anybody. On the contrary, I do a little good whenever I can — it is my only pleasure."

(Letter from RIMBAUD
to his mother
— February 25, 1890)

"En effet, il est défendu à l'homme, sous peine de déchéance et de mort intellectuelle, de déranger les conditions primordiales de son existence et de rompre l'équilibre de ses facultés avec les milieux où elles sont destinées à se mouvoir, de déranger son destin pour y substituer une fatalité d'un genre nouveau. Tout homme qui n'accepte pas les conditions de sa vie vend son âme."

BAUDELAIRE

"I always carry over 40,000 gold francs about with me in my belt. They weigh about forty pounds and I am beginning to get dysentery from the load."

RIMBAUD
(Letter to his mother.)

444 Ocampo Drive
Pacific Palisades, California
July 9, 1973

Dear Michel:

I finally finished reading the letters — took me several sessions. What an adventure! When you first broached the subject I was skeptical, but after reading them I am enthusiastic. Too bad you didn't send me yours to read also. You will notice I made very few cuts; I left the Paul Weiss passages in.

About a third of the way through I began cutting the quotes around book titles and underlying [sic] them instead. Also underlined all French words. These should be italicized, no?

The letters from Lepska are beautiful. But should they be in the body of the text, or put at the end of the book separately? I notice big gaps in later years. Have you withheld some of my letters or did I not write you during these periods?

What pleases me very much about them is that they have so much to do with literature — and almost exclusively French literature. I forgot that I had read some of the authors mentioned. I begin to wonder if this correspondence would not be better coming out in French first. As for U.S., there is the Grove Press — Barney Rosset, who put up such a fight to save me from the censors. The worst publishers, as I told you before, are the University Presses. They are dead wood.

I went into the other room to get something and there was Lepska talking to Tony, who is going to get married shortly. I told her I was just writing you. She sends warm regards.

I send the MS. separately, either registered or insured. Let me hear from you soon. Sorry I delayed so long, but it was unavoidable.

All the best now.

Henry

Index

Abélard, Pierre, 69
Abramson, Ben, 54
Adriani, 112
Apollinaire, Guillaume, 87, 121, 127
Artaud, Antonin, 132

Bach, Johann Sebastian, 168
Bacon, Sir Francis, 77, 85
Balzac, Honoré de, 63, 92, 97, 129, 136, 165, 166
Barnes, Djuna, 12
Baudelaire, Charles, 17, 87, 91, 118, 145, 167, 169, 173
Bauer, Maria, 77, 85
Beckett, Samuel, 16
Bédier, Joseph, 44, 46
Belgion, Montgomery, 146
Belitt, Ben, 112
Belloc, Hilaire, 46
Belmont, Georges, 13, 14, 158
Berdyaev, Nikolai, 153
Bernanos, Georges, 53, 57
Berrichon, Paterne, 71

Blackwood, Algernon, 66
Blake, William, 167
Bloy, Léon, 61, 82, 99, 102, 119
Boehme, Jacob, 172
Bogan, Louise, 146
Bosch, Hieronymus, 18
Brassai, 14, 84
Breton, André, 11, 49, 121
Bruckberger, Père, 115, 133, 136, 139, 140
Buchanan, Harvey, 8, 72, 79, 80

Cain, Julien, 123
Calas, Nicolas, 23
Camus, Albert, 87, 88, 93, 149
Carco, Francis, 83, 86, 88, 91
Carrington, Lenora, 49
Cartier-Bresson, Henri, 127
Cayton, Horace, 127
Cebulski, Frank, 150
Céline, Louis-Ferdinand, 8, 64, 169, 171
Cendrars, Blaise, 8, 134, 135, 137, 139, 165, 169